To Be a Servant-Leader

TO BE A
SERVANT-LEADER

Stephen Prosser

PAULIST PRESS
New York/Mahwah, NJ

Cover design by Sharyn Banks
Book design by Lynn Else

Library of Congress Cataloging-in-Publication Data

Prosser, Stephen.
    To be a servant-leader / Stephen Prosser.
        p. cm.
    Includes bibliographical references.
    ISBN 978–0–8091–4467–9 (alk. paper)
    1. Christian leadership. 2. Service (Theology) I. Title.
    BV652.1.P76 2007
    253—dc22

                                                            2006037764

Published by Paulist Press
997 Macarthur Boulevard
Mahwah, New Jersey 07430

www.paulistpress.com

Printed and bound in the
United States of America

Contents

For Lesley

Preface

Earlier this year I looked in my diary and to my horror discovered that I had absolutely nothing to do for the next three days. There were no meetings, my pile of reading had been eliminated, I had answered all of my e-mails and messages, the next round of consultancy assignments and meetings were not until the following week, and, best of all, the final draft of my latest manuscript was winging its way to the publisher. I had nothing to do! Absolutely nothing.

Instead of listening to my wife's sage advice to relax, go for a walk, do some thinking—how wise she is—watch a film, or paint the fence, believe it or not I started to fret: *I've got nothing to do!* The workaholic in me was becoming more than a little anxious.

Suddenly, it dawned on me: *I know what I can do*. It was something I had wanted to do for ages. As a professor of leadership and someone actively involved in promoting servant-leadership, I had wanted free time to find out what the Bible had to say about the topic of leadership, and servant-leadership in particular. Please don't stop reading this preface just because you saw the word *Bible*, since the remainder of the preface, and the rest of the book, make it perfectly clear that this is a book on servant-leadership for everyone—"for people of all faiths or people of no faith," as they say—although, inevitably, there is an added incentive for those who want to ensure that their daily life is compatible with the teaching of the Bible.

So I set out on my voyage of discovery to see what the "Old Book" had to say and when I took the words *leader, leadership, leading, led, manager, overseer,* and many others, and fed them into an online concordance, out came hundreds of references. I had to reduce them to a manageable number, by a process that's far too routine to describe in detail here, and I ended up with a list of around one hundred references. In the end, these became what I went on to call my "solid references." Eventually, some overlapping themes were eliminated and the total of solid references was whittled down even further to seventy-nine. These references are included in the appendix, together with a brief description of the text to assist the reader's understanding of the context.

Painstakingly, I started reading them to identify their context and to make sure that I understood what they had to say about leadership. I made some notes on my laptop computer and then something happened that really surprised me: As I started to write down what I had intended to be a sentence or two about each of the references, words began to flow out of me. The quotes and references were acting as a trigger, as a catalyst, for numerous thoughts about servant-leadership, about the leaders and about those being led.

A seemingly passing reference to leadership in the text would result in four hundred words or so appearing on my laptop screen. A reference to a decidedly dodgy woman and a suspect king in the Old Testament saw me writing three hundred words on corporate governance and accountability. Words of guidance to a young leader in the New Testament became qualities for servant-leaders to aspire to two thousand years later. Also, at times my initial style of writing appeared to be reminiscent of a management textbook of a former era or, as one friend helpfully observed, in a medieval style approaching that of the Rule of St. Benedict. It was a strange experience and the initial three days of study turned into three months of writing.

Professional theologians would be rightly offended if I presented the source references and findings, and the thoughts based on them, and claimed that somehow I was expounding the real meaning of the original Hebrew or Greek texts. Most definitely, I am not. What follows is not an exposition of the text—rather, what follows is a stream of thoughts about servant-leadership that were inspired by what I read, and, while the thoughts are based on reliable principles (in my opinion), they are certainly not infallible thoughts! Neither am I claiming that every possible biblical reference to servant-leadership has been picked up; I may well have omitted some references for what appears to be entirely subjective reasons. Therefore, readers may well exclaim, "Why hasn't he included the reference in..." or even "How on earth could he interpret that to mean...." All I can say in response, or even in defense, is that I wrote about what challenged me and I am sure that these thoughts will challenge you equally. I want to emphasize that what is presented has been designed to make you think about leadership. If it does that, and helps you improve your leadership practice, then the authority of my words is not important. What matters is that the words have helped you to improve your leadership practice.

There are two further points to make concerning the source references. First, I have left out quite intentionally all references to Jesus and his leadership style, since many first-class books have been written on that topic and because people reading this book might look at his supreme example and say, "How can I emulate him? He was the Son of God, wasn't he?" The second point concerns some overlaps in the text: While I have done my utmost to keep these overlaps to an absolute minimum, inevitably some remain that I hope the charitable reader will interpret as an opportunity to reinforce a particular point, just as the Old and New Testament do on many occasions.

As I explored the text, the various servant-leadership ideas began to coalesce into six distinct headings:

1. The Nature and Qualities of Servant-Leadership
2. The Work of a Servant-Leader
3. The Appointment of Servant-Leaders and the Question of Succession
4. Servant-Leadership and Management
5. Servant-Leadership and Followers
6. When Leadership Goes Wrong (In this section I consider leadership in the broadest sense of the term.)

When the first draft of my thoughts had been prepared, I decided to test the water. I identified nine present or former colleagues, some of whom are close friends, and sent them an e-mail containing my draft. I am not suggesting that my friends, colleagues, and ex-colleagues are a representative cross section of society—for one thing they were all men—but they are expert in leadership and they represent a group of people whose judgment and experience could be trusted. I also knew from past experience that they would be kind enough to tell me if they thought that what I had written would be useful for a wider audience, or whether the material would be of little use. I sat back and awaited their response.

Their responses arrived in a surprisingly short space of time. They were encouraging and included comments such as:

> I think this says some very important things and brings them together in a way that really sharpens their impact. I think it's important work and I'm really thrilled that it's being done.
>
> I also like the structure—the way you've broken down the components and the order of them is very helpful and would make it a very useable handbook.
>
> I also like it because it's a look at leadership which is as useful to the led as to those who are or would be leaders.
>
> Can I say immediately that I think this is a hugely important contribution to our "spirituality of organisations" agenda because it has focus, authority, and challenge.
>
> The paper contains an amazingly rich variety of material. It is good to see the moral and ethical emphasis to a lot of the material, not just technical.

But they all thought that the first draft contained far too many ideas compressed into long and complex paragraphs that were far too heavy to digest in one sitting. One of my colleagues came up with the perfect metaphor to describe the draft when he wrote: "My main point is this: It's a bit like trying to eat a whole Stilton.* Stilton has a strong and very intense taste. Although I really like it, I can only have a few slices at a time. Your document is tasty, but very intense. Individual paragraphs are full of good content, but reading more than a few, leaves me feeling very 'full.'"

---

* For those not familiar with the joy of eating Stilton, it is a strong-tasting and rich English cheese.

I hasten to add that subsequent drafts—and this final version of the manuscript—have had the indigestible parts taken out and the feeling of congestion and complexity has been removed.

However, *a whole Stilton* remains a most suitable metaphor. This volume is intended to provide you with a number of tasty servant-leadership morsels to chew on, to think about, and, I hope, to digest. It does not matter whether you agree with everything I have written. Whether you agree is not the point; the point of the volume is to encourage you to ponder the principle of servant-leadership and to convert your thoughts into actions that are meaningful and digestible for you.

Let me tell you a secret: I'm not sure that I've worked out yet how all of these servant-leadership principles can be applied in practice, but they have most definitely caused me to think profoundly about how I perform my leadership role...and that is the purpose of this book.

Stephen Prosser
Llandeilo, Wales
May 2006.

*"And whosoever will be chief among you,
let him be your servant."*

Matthew 20:27 (King James Version)

I
Introduction

Identifying, presenting, and examining evidence, from whatever source, to illuminate and further understand the origins and meanings of servant-leadership was a practice that found favor time and again with Robert Greenleaf, the person rightly credited with introducing the concept of servant-leadership into twentieth- and twenty-first century thought. For example, in *Lessons on Power*[1] Greenleaf wrote:

> In our Western tradition, from the Old Testament prophets down to now, there is a vast store of wisdom that is relevant to times of crisis like ours when the reckless use of power threatens society and the people who should speak with one voice about right and wrong are in a babel of confusion. I have not reviewed all of our store of wisdom by far, but I assure you that in the last couple of years, I have been spurred to a much larger than usual preoccupation with the great wisdom sources. *Where else, really, can we go?* [my italics]

Robert K. Greenleaf (1904–1990) achieved iconic status among organizational and leadership thinkers, educators, business and nonprofit organizations, and far beyond. Peter Drucker, the greatest of the management gurus, called Greenleaf "the wisest man I ever met." As Greenleaf's story is explained in most books on servant-leadership, I shall confine myself to explaining the key events in the development of his thinking. Following university, he joined AT&T, where he specialized in management research, development, and education and spent many years reflecting on

3

issues of leadership and effectiveness within organizations. His extensive reading included Hermann Hesse's novel *Journey to the East*, and it was while reading of how Leo, the servant to a group of people on a mythical journey, provided an essential leadership role and became the guiding spirit of the group that Greenleaf's thinking on leadership crystallized: He began to understand the significance of the leader as servant, that is, he began to see leadership as an act of servanthood.

At the age of sixty-six Greenleaf wrote *The Servant as Leader*[2] and over the years its sales, and more importantly its influence on people and organizations, have made it something of a publishing phenomenon. The book contains his central thesis, his description of servant-leadership, and it poses a stimulating challenge:

> It begins with the natural feeling that one wants to serve, to serve first. Then conscious choice brings one to aspire to lead. The best test is: do those served grow as persons; do they, while being served, become healthier, wiser, freer, more autonomous, more likely themselves to become servants? And, what is the effect on the least privileged in society: will they benefit, or at least, not be further deprived?

This became his inspiration and the driving force behind his belief that leadership should be based on the concept of the leader, the servant-leader, being *primus inter pares*—the first among equals—and this belief resulted in a series of challenging essays, speeches, and articles that have stood the test of time. Many of his essays are not the easiest of reads—he was in many ways a philosopher and polemicist—but the following quotations from his work illustrate the depth of his ideas:

The great leader is seen as servant first.

Leaders do not elicit trust unless one has confidence in their values and competence and unless they have a sustaining spirit that will support the tenacious pursuit of a goal.

I am in the business of growing people—people who are stronger, healthier, more autonomous, more self-reliant, more competent....

It is quite easy to fall into the trap of reading some of Greenleaf's writings and thinking of him as a dewy-eyed dreamer with little relevance to business in the twenty-first century; but such an assessment is quite erroneous. Not only have Greenleaf's writings influenced many of the most noted organizational writers, but also many successful companies and public organizations today practice his beliefs. As I show in chapter 3, where I explain my surprising discovery of servant-leadership and my commitment to its principles, successful business practice and servant-leadership are certainly not incompatible.

Anyone who has read Greenleaf's writings extensively will also be impressed by the comprehensive way in which he drew inspiration from poets, philosophers, various scholars, students, writers, and, of course, managers, academics, and trustees for his expanding thoughts on servant-leadership. Some of the major sources for reflection in his writings were accounts taken from the Old and New Testaments. One well-known Greenleaf story, told in his own words in *The Servant Leader Within*,[3] illustrates this:

> Shortly after the first essay was published, a Catholic Sister...came to talk about it. In the course of the conversation, she asked me where, in literature, I found the first reference to servant? My reply was, "In the Bible, all through the Bible. I checked the concordance and found 1,300 references." "Why then," was her sharp question, "do you attribute what you have written to Hermann Hesse?" "Because," I replied, "that is where I got the idea of 'The Servant as Leader.'"

Greenleaf's ongoing fascination with biblical accounts is shown throughout his writings. In *Seeker and Servant*[4] he wrote:

> The idea of servant is deep within our Judeo-Christian heritage. Servant (along with serve and service) appears

in the Bible more than thirteen hundred times. Part of the human dilemma is that the meaning of serve, in practical behavioural terms for both persons and institutions, is never completely clear. Thus one who would be servant is a life-long seeker, groping for light but never finding ultimate clarity. One constantly probes and listens, both to the promptings from one's own inner resources and to the communications of those who are also seeking. Then one cautiously experiments, questions, and listens again. Thus the servant-seeker is constantly growing in self-assurance through experience, but never having the solace of certainty.

His published private writings return many times to such themes. In *The Practice of Openness*,[5] for example, he uses an account from the New Testament (the woman taken in adultery) to illustrate his principle of dealing with contentious issues; in *Entheos and Growth*[6] he uses another New Testament story (Martha and Mary) to illustrate one of his misleading indicators about *entheos* (possessed by the spirit in a positive constructive sense), namely *busyness*. In *Coercion, Manipulation, and Persuasion*[7] he uses another New Testament event (the money changers in the Temple) to illustrate the difference between persuasion and coercion.

In *Entheos and Growth*, and also in *Authority and Strength: The Problem of Power*,[8] Robert Greenleaf draws heavily on the story of Moses and his father-in-law, Jethro. Moses had become exhausted dealing with the problems brought to him by the people he was leading. Thinking that Jethro's advice contained a fatal flaw concerning the structure of leadership and the use of power, Greenleaf goes on to argue for the use of leadership by persuasion and example as the way to build effectively. It may be that Greenleaf did not have too much sympathy for Moses, as once more he uses Moses to demonstrate "the all too common fault (in the Western world) of settling for mediocrity" and he sees this as deriving "from a flaw that is right at the heart of traditional moral law." Greenleaf tells the story of Moses receiving the Ten Commandments, "chiselled in stone and bearing God's imprimatur" (what a wonderful Greenleaf phrase), and regrets that Moses presented the Law as something from on high rather than presenting it "as a reasonable codification of experience and wisdom, a summary of those sensible rules to guide individual conduct and as the basis for a good society."

You do not have to agree with Greenleaf's exegesis of the Bible to appreciate the extent to which he drew on these Bible narratives to illustrate principles of servant-leadership. Therefore, it is surely legitimate for us to follow suit; perhaps it even behooves us to imitate the practice of Greenleaf himself and to examine historical records, literature, and the practices of a variety of institutions to help deepen our understanding of servant-leadership and to promulgate its practice to others. Deep within that search stand the writings of the Bible, and it is interesting to note the extent to which biblical passages have inspired other writers on servant-leadership.

Ken Blanchard, a leading management thinker, in *The Heart of Servant-Leadership*[9] demonstrates this inspiration:

> [T]he concepts I had learned from Greenleaf did not return to centre stage in my work until the mid 1990s, when I began studying Jesus of Nazareth as a clear example of enlightened leadership...when I started to read the Bible, I began to realise that everything I'd ever taught about leadership over the years, Jesus had already modelled. Jesus is not only a spiritual model, but his leadership style is often regarded as one of the most influential and effective the world has ever known...and central to Jesus' philosophy was servant-leadership. I believe Jesus exemplified the fully committed and effective servant-leader.

And in *Servant-Leadership Revisited*[10] Blanchard uses Jesus' leadership style as the basis for much of this article. He concludes with a telling point that emphasizes that servant-leadership is committed to the overall direction of the organization: "...the essence of Jesus' servant-leadership symbolised in the washing of his disciples' feet only began once his vision and direction were clear."

James A. Autry, the successful businessman and advocate of servant-leadership, in *The Servant Leader*[11] highlights the connection between servant-leadership and spirituality within the workplace:

I say "the spirit of work" to distinguish your spirituality at work from the more personal spirituality that comes from your relationship with the sacred, with God, with a higher power. Certainly the spirituality you bring to work is derived from the same source—but the expression of it is in another context, which is "How does your spirituality find expression in the workplace, in your attitude about your work, in your relationships with your employees, peers, colleagues, customers, vendors and others?" That's the question and the challenge, because it is in your attitude and behaviour as well as in your relationships that your spirituality expresses itself at work—an expression that is most often manifest as service.

In *Love and Profit: The Art of Caring Leadership*,[12] Autry discusses the ideal workplace, as reflected in many books about renewal in the workplace, and he makes the telling comment:

> And in this workplace, everyone is treated with dignity and respect, with honesty and trust, and with love—the values and qualities that will make business better even when business is not going well.
> I think that's the kind of business Jesus would run. We could call it Christian business; we could call it humanistic business; we could call it smart business.
> Whatever we call it, it sounds like heaven to me.

Many other writers follow a similar track. Bill Bottum and Dorothy Lenz's *Within Our Reach: Servant-Leadership for the Twenty-first Century*,[13] for example, sets out their view of "Guiding Principles for Business Based on the Beatitudes" and then demonstrates its link to servant-leadership. David L. Specht, with Richard R. Brohom, in *Toward a Theology of Institutions*,[14] respond to Greenleaf's call for a theology of institutions with their "Four Theological Premises for Those Who Would Hold Organizations in Trust." In *Tracing the Vision and Impact of Robert K. Greenleaf*,[15] Joseph J. DiStefano also acknowledges Greenleaf's institutional and theological view. And Carl Rieser, in *Claiming Servant-Leadership as*

Your Heritage,[16] discusses the role and place of a servant millennia ago by drawing on the evidence of the Book of Leviticus and the Year of Jubilee.

Therefore, from Greenleaf himself and from numerous other writers, far too many to mention, a clear precedent can be seen in drawing inspiration and thereby further insight into servant-leadership from many sources, including the Bible.

Anyone with an interest in the theories of leadership will know that the world is awash with books on the subject. As I write these words, the bookshelves in front of me contain leadership books telling the reader about *Authentic, Empowered, Primal, Strategic, Charismatic, Transformational, Inspiring, Collaborative, Extraordinary,* and *Complete* leadership, and just about every other adjective, verb, and noun you can imagine to capture different dimensions of the leadership role. Perhaps the most apt book title is *Leadership Without Easy Answers.*[17] That seems to sum up leadership: It is an enormously complex subject and that is why anyone who attempts to reduce leadership to a few glib words, or a clever-sounding phrase, is worthy of being intellectually hanged, drawn, and quartered. Leadership is difficult to understand and it is even more difficult to practice and so further insights into the theory and practice of servant-leadership, from whatever quarter, should be welcomed.

This book provides such an insight. What follows will provoke thought and debate, contention and argument, and will encourage personal reflection. This book will also help you to take an informed yet open view of the intriguing concept of servant-leadership, red in tooth and claw, because it reveals both the successes and pleasures of being a servant-leader and also some of the challenges and difficulties.

The various sections have been set out in chunk-bite sizes. My advice to you is that you shouldn't try to read the entire book in one or two sittings. The volume is intended as something you can dip into, discuss with your colleagues, think about, agree or disagree with, and then put to one side until the next time you want something to provoke your thinking about your role as a servant-leader.

Many books and articles on servant-leadership, written by highly regarded people, have been written either by individuals examining the principles of servant-leadership generally or, and more likely, by those who work for organizations where the principles of servant-leadership are practiced throughout the organization. Where this book differs is that it also addresses the role of individual servant-leaders who may operate in organizations that adopt an antithetical position to servant-leadership, and perhaps even react to its principles with a degree of hostility. Yet, these brave souls who continue to fly the flag for servant-leadership within their hostile organizations will find much in the book to encourage them and help them think about how they should continue to act.

Another difference in this book is that it recognizes that it is possible for a servant-leadership organization to experience substantial adverse business conditions. Adopting servant-leadership principles, while significantly aiding the success of an organization, does not automatically inure the organization from the realities of the marketplace or the potential misdemeanors of individuals. There are organizations—admittedly not ones openly espousing servant-leadership principles but nonetheless ones that have followed a similar set of principles for decades—that have experienced traumatic times, and therefore this book also raises issues concerning the role of leadership when things go wrong.

Small businesses often experience difficulties when the founder and first CEO of the organization decides to retire and the issue of succession, dealt with in this book, becomes a significant issue. The same issues can arise in the larger organization when the CEO, who may well have been the principal advocate for servant-leadership, decides to stand down and a replacement has to be found.

In addition, and for those who are fairly new to the concept of servant-leadership, I have introduced a chapter that explains why I am committed to its principles. The chapter is based on previous writings[18] and addresses I delivered at the Greenleaf Servant-Leadership UK Conference in 2002 and at the University of Oxford in 2005.

Consider what the various chapters have to say. Without doubt, they will cause you to think; they might even infuriate you; they will certainly make you examine your own leadership style and beliefs. You may even end up asking: "Is this leadership? Can leadership really be like this?" If that is your reaction then I have been successful in my objective.

Robert Greenleaf, in *Servant Leadership: A Journey into the Nature of Legitimate Power and Greatness*,[19] considered the need for "prophetic voices in our midst" and he wrote:

> I now embrace the theory of prophecy which holds that prophetic voices of great clarity, and with a quality of insight equal to that of any age, are speaking cogently all the time....
>
> It is seekers, then, who make prophets, and the initiative of any one of us in searching for and responding to the voice of contemporary prophets may mark the turning point in their growth and service.... We listen to as wide a range of contemporary thought as we can attend to. Then we choose those we elect to heed as prophets— both old and new—and meld their advice with our own leadings. This we test in real-life experiences to establish our own position....
>
> One does not, of course, ignore the great voices of the past. One does not awaken each morning with the compulsion to reinvent the wheel. But if one is servant, either leader or follower, one is always searching, listening, expecting that a better wheel for these times is in the making.

Greenleaf reminds us that it is the seeker who may one day become the prophet. Let me wish you every success in your search.

II

Appropriate Servant-Leadership Characteristics

The Nature and Qualities of Servant-Leadership

Attitudes

The attitude of a servant-leader will be that of a shepherd: someone who will exercise care as well as lead, someone who will protect as well as guide.

The servant-leader will see leadership as a form of service to other people and undertake the responsibilities willingly, not through compulsion, or grudgingly, or by reason of self-interest. Servant-leadership is an act that will benefit other people as much, if not more, than the leader him- or herself.

The servant-leader will not consider the position of leader to be a reason to adopt a superior attitude to those being led.

Younger leaders should pay respect to those who are older, wiser, and far more experienced than they. Humility is an attractive quality in all people but especially in those who are young and naïve about so many things in life. Humble leaders achieve far more than proud leaders, even if it does not appear to be the case in the short term.

Being anxious is an unhelpful state of mind. Servant-leaders who experience anxiety should find someone to confide in, someone whose experience and wise counsel can help the servant-leaders overcome their anxiety and, if at all possible, learn from their experience.

Servant-leaders exhibit self-control so that, among other things, they may be alert to people who intend to cause the servant-leader problems and difficulties. These people can be resisted by standing fast to one's principles and by realizing that other servant-leaders face similar challenges as a test of their leadership; this realization is best arrived at by accepting the advice of more-experienced leaders. These challenges, while unpleasant when they occur, can actually make the leader stronger and more secure over time.

The servant-leader will never lead when financial gain is the major motivation and should realize that there are far greater rewards available to effective leaders than those linked to mere financial benefits.

REFERENCE 1 (IN APPENDIX)

Questions

1. If a servant-leader behaves as a shepherd, and as someone who sees leadership as a service to others, how does the servant-leader ensure that those being led do not exploit the chosen style of leadership?
2. How does the servant-leader achieve the right balance between encouraging young leaders to be bold while at the same time ensuring that they are humbly aware of their relative inexperience?
3. Why is it essential for a servant-leader to have access to someone who can offer wise advice?

Vision

A servant-leader will have a clear sense of vision and that vision must be the driving force in all actions that are undertaken. The vision should excite the servant-leader, it should be a motivational force, and the leader's belief in the vision should be clear for all to see. The servant-leader will be under no misapprehension that his or her demeanor is being observed at all times by the people being led and they will be aware whether the leader really believes in the declared vision.

The vision needs to be communicated to other leaders and, for those in the enterprise who are less interested in the vision itself and more interested in what the vision means for their work, the vision should be interpreted into a clear set of objectives and instructions. There are people of vision and there are people of action: Both types of people must feel satisfied, as both types of people are valuable, even indispensable, to the organization.

Unfortunately, there are some so-called leaders who do not possess real vision. They are adept at saying the words they know people in authority want to hear, but they do not believe these words in their innermost being. They utter the words in an attempt to impress those they believe can prosper or advance their careers some time in the future. But people know that what they hear from this type of leader are words alone and that in their hearts are other views, perhaps contrary views, or even no views at all. They merely utter words, words they do not even believe. They are people without vision.

The servant-leader is the complete opposite of such a visionless person.

REFERENCES 2-3

Questions

1. How can a servant-leader's vision be translated into something that is meaningful for all groups of people within the organization, so that they too are motivated toward the achievement of the vision?
2. How should a servant-leader react to other leaders who have no real vision and merely utter platitudes with little meaning?

Example

Principally, the practice of servant-leadership is based on the leader acting as a model or example to those being led, and servant-leaders will be wholeheartedly committed to those they lead.

Servant-leaders will ensure that they are able to understand their own behaviors (the issues that motivate them and those that frustrate them), the nature of their organization, and the characteristics of the people they have the privilege to lead. In order to achieve this, servant-leaders will be practiced in reflection on how to gain valuable insights into their own behavior and that of others. In this way they will be able to decide, even discern through their knowledge, reflection, and resulting intuition, the most appropriate courses of action.

In all things, and especially in their successes, servant-leaders will be ready to praise other people more than themselves for the achievements obtained in their organizations.

To be the leader of people is a great honor and privilege and should not be approached lightly or offhandedly. The servant-leader, as an example to others, will be beyond reproach in all aspects of life: in terms of family affairs, in personal behavior and self-control, as a respected member of the community, in dealings with people at work and at home, and in being approachable rather than argumentative and vindictive.

Servant-leaders will set this example and ensure that no parts of their life can be the cause of contention; otherwise, the credibility of their leadership will be tarnished. In the conduct of their personal business they will ensure that actions are, and are seen to be, upright and free of censure. If someone cannot lead a life that is respected by others, then how is that person expected to lead others honorably?

A servant-leader should not be immature or inexperienced, or the person may develop too great an opinion of him- or herself or may be deceived by those with far greater experience.

At all levels in the organization these principles should be the model of leadership. Newly appointed leaders should undergo a trial period during which their abilities and commitment are tested. Only after they have been tested, and, prior to that, given suitable assistance to make their mark, should they be confirmed as servant-leaders. To be a servant-leader is to accept a position of substantial responsibility and therefore it is right that the demands placed upon leaders, in terms of how they conduct their lives, should be equally demanding.

REFERENCES 4–5

Questions

1. To what extent are the actions of a servant-leader observed and analyzed by "followers"?
2. Is regular and systematic reflection a practice that allows the servant-leader to understand how those being led see him or her?
3. Can the actions and conduct of a servant-leader, within and outside the workplace, have a substantial impact upon those being led? Or should the servant-leader's personal life be of no concern to those within the organization?

Respect

A servant-leader will treat everyone with respect and use exhortation, far more than criticism, when speaking to those in his or her charge. The relationship between the servant-leader and those being led will be based on sensitivity rather than harshness.

The servant-leader will recognize the talents and the needs of those around him or her and pay particular regard to the balance between work and family responsibilities.

Those being led have an equal responsibility to respect the leader. Servant-leaders who lead well should be honored for their work and rewarded accordingly; those being led should also be rewarded fairly.

If complaints are brought against a servant-leader, they should be treated urgently and seriously. Unsubstantiated complaints against a leader should be handled with caution to ensure that everyone is treated fairly and that a servant-leader is not burdened by scurrilous accusations.

A servant-leader will lead without partiality to any one person or group of people and do nothing out of favoritism. Most decisions should not be made hastily, and a servant-leader should gain a reputation for the good things that are done and not for those that bring shame on the organization.

While servant-leaders should be respected, they also must realize that respect has to be earned. The servant-leader will not be conceited and will not be the type of person known to like controversy and pedantry, for this is likely to generate dissent, suspicion, and friction.

The servant-leader will be wary of people who are committed solely to financial gain, as they are likely to be open to unacceptable behavior.

The servant-leader will possess personal qualities that are admired and will ensure that he or she is not: overbearing in the demands made of others; quick-tempered, especially when judgments have to be made; apt to lose control; discourteous in the way they treat others; or interested in pursuing objectives considered to be improper.

The servant-leader will have a welcoming attitude toward others and will attract others as a result of his or her reputation for honorable behavior, for being upright in all actions, and for expecting everyone to conduct themselves ethically.

Servant-leaders will adhere to the mission of the enterprise without compromise, encourage others to do likewise, and oppose those who attempt to undermine the mission.

The servant-leader will ensure that immediate action is taken against rebellious people; otherwise, their actions will spoil the potential existing within other parts of the organization.

No one should be allowed to profit through dishonest gain, and anyone contemplating or undertaking such behavior should be rebuked strongly. Where such action has no or little effect, these dishonorable people should be excluded from the organization.

Servant-leaders will be teachers showing all other people the ways in which they should conduct themselves.

REFERENCES 6–7

Questions

1. Does respect have to be earned or should it be automatically given to the servant-leader because of the post that is

held? And why should the servant-leader actively respect those who work for him or her?

2. If a complaint is made against a servant-leader, what are the key factors that should govern the way in which the complaint is handled? Is it possible to deal with these matters speedily?

3. What personal qualities is it essential for a servant-leader to possess?

Change and Counsel

A wise servant-leader will understand that one person cannot accomplish everything and that leadership is best shared with others. When a servant-leader experiences leadership becoming a burden, he or she should speak to someone older and wiser and seek advice. The wiser person will show the younger or less-experienced servant-leader that:

1. to continue with the present workload will result in exhaustion;

2. the servant-leader should choose to concentrate effort on key issues;

3. other servant-leaders should be appointed who are capable, perhaps after appropriate training, of handling all other issues.

As the other servant-leaders share the burden, the leader will be able "to stand the strain."

Some new servant-leaders are capable of looking after the needs of a large number of people, while others may only be able to look after the needs of a small number at first.

No leader is indispensable, and a shared and distributed model of servant-leadership makes everyone more effective.

A servant-leader realizes that changing circumstances may require new principles and instructions to be developed and issued. It is often the case that even the best-developed plans have not anticipated all potential sets of circumstances, and a wise servant-leader is always open to suggestions that things should be changed. Certainly, the servant-leader will be humble enough to accept that not every contingency had been considered in the first place. When such changes take place, the new arrangements should be made clear and the reasons for the change should be explained fully to the people affected by the change.

As an organization becomes more successful and increases in size, the pressure on the servant-leader will grow, and unless action is taken it may become intolerable. Success brings change and this change may even be in the very style of leadership. When this happens, it should be explained to the people involved that there is a need to change both the way work is organized and the way in which they are to be led.

At times it may be wise to involve people in choosing the leaders they wish to lead them and to ask them to identify potential servant-leaders who possess sufficient wisdom, understanding, and respect. Appointing deputy leaders who are seen as being representative of people in the organization can have merit.

There are times when it is necessary for the servant-leaders of the organization to meet, away from their place of work, to reconsider their vision and their commitment to it. There is a need for the servant-leaders to remind one another of the importance of their vision to all that they do and to agree on what each leader will achieve in order to ensure that the vision remains a reality within their organization.

Sometimes there is a need to determine the extent to which the vision is still driving the actions of each servant-leader and to ensure that, where there are deficiencies, the vision has been refreshed in each servant-leader. In this way the vision will continue to be a shared and dynamic one and no single leader will have to carry the responsibility alone.

Servant-leaders will act cautiously with people, including some other leaders, who express a view that it was "better in the old days"—the days before the current vision was accepted as the driving force for the organization—for they may be people who laud the so-called better days in order to cover up their inability to deliver the requirements of the new vision. Or they may be the type of people who lose heart much more easily and so become negative in their assessment of work.

REFERENCES 8–11

Questions

1. Why is it important for a servant-leader to practice what has been called distributive leadership, that is, involving many people in the task of leadership?
2. When an organization expands in size, or when there is a need to significantly alter the direction being taken by the organization, what are the key factors for the servant-leader to bear in mind?
3. What are the substantive differences between checking regularly that the vision of the organization remains relevant and questioning the vision in a way that suggests a lack of confidence in it?

Reward

Successful servant-leaders should be rewarded generously for the results they have achieved and for the continuous responsibilities they are prepared to carry.

Competitors may attempt to take away an organization's leaders in order to enhance their own position and inflict harm on the other organization. It is important that valued servant-leaders are protected from the attacks of unscrupulous organizations and, also, that servant-leaders feel that genuine offers from other organizations can be considered quite openly and without any sense that it will be seen as an act of disloyalty.

Each organization must have a range of talents and gifts if it is to function effectively. Servant-leadership should be seen as one of these gifts. It is a precious gift and should be handled with great care. Although the practice of servant-leadership can be learned, there are some who have the distinct advantages of being born with many of the inherent qualities. Such people have an even greater responsibility to lead well.

REFERENCES 12–15

Questions

1. How important is it to reward servant-leaders generously while not creating an impression, in others, that the amounts being paid cannot be justified?
2. How does an organization set about identifying those with servant-leadership potential?
3. How should a servant-leader react when a competitor organization makes an attractive offer of employment?

The Work of a Servant-Leader

The Wider Responsibilities

Individual leaders realize that they belong to a wider community of servant-leaders within their organizations and, therefore, have a responsibility for local activities and people, and also for activities at the national or international level. Servant-leaders demonstrate an acceptance of the larger organization and a willingness to play a significant part in national activities, which may include funding certain national activities from income held locally. The servant-leader will recognize the value and contribution of leadership at different levels in the organization.

There are times when a fellow servant-leader experiences extremely difficult times in his or her personal life or in the place of work. Other servant-leaders will do their best to support the leader experiencing these difficult times since they realize that such action is both compassionate and sensible, as the day will come when they may need similar support from their colleagues.

Servant-leaders never make use of times of challenge, experienced by another leader, as an opportunity to advance their own cause or to harm the future prospects of their colleague. Such action and scheming is deprecated by servant-leaders.

All servant-leaders will do their utmost to nurture their leadership role and to develop their performance within the role, especially where they believe they have a natural gift for leadership. They see servant-leadership as extremely important and give themselves to it wholeheartedly. As they become better servant-leaders, their own leaders, including those who appointed them, and those being led by them will observe the progress they are making and be pleased.

REFERENCES 16–18

Questions

1. How can servant-leaders be helped if they have a tendency to take an insular view of their leadership responsibilities?
2. What provisions should be set in place to help servant-leaders who are experiencing challenging times in their personal lives?
3. What are the most effective ways to develop a servant-leader?

Developing Policy

When major decisions have to be made, it is important to gather as much information as possible before the decision is taken and appropriate policies, strategies, and tactics are devised. One of the more successful ways of accumulating the necessary information and intelligence is to appoint representatives from all parts of the organization to investigate the opportunities that are available. When these representatives are appointed, they should be given clear guidance concerning what is expected of them, no aspect of their investigation should be left to chance, and they should know the time set for their investigation and final report. Suitable mechanisms should also be set in place to enable them to undertake their tasks according to plan.

When the representatives present their report, it is essential to discover the views of each of the persons involved in the investigation. Sometimes a report can be distorted by the fact that it has been based on a majority view, or a compromise among the various members of the group, when in fact the minority view is by far the most sensible.

It should be remembered that some people enjoy hearing their own voice in a room full of people, and there are times when the quieter voice, or the person who chooses to speak last, has far more common sense and mature judgment to communicate than certain members of the team. The servant-leader ensures that all views are aired and that such a practice is seen as part of how a wise organization acts.

The servant-leader will also be aware that some members of the investigation are more timid and cautious than others and that some colleagues are more likely to suggest adventurous alternatives. Therefore, all suggestions should be weighed carefully.

Unfortunately, there are times when those who hold a particular alternative view will attempt to make their view succeed by persuading other people within the organization. By spreading rumors they can cause widespread concern and discontent and may make decision making harder. A servant-leader acts firmly to show that messages given by such dissenters are incorrect and misleading.

Once a decision has been made, care must be taken to ensure that as many people as possible understand the decision fully and give it their support. Then actions should be put in place to implement the decision as speedily as possible. Colleagues who were courageous enough to express a minority view, a view that was seen by all eventually to be the wisest course of action, should be rewarded accordingly and their expertise should be used in the future.

REFERENCE 19

Questions

1. How feasible and desirable is it to involve as many people as possible, from all parts and levels of the organization, in the development of policy, and can a servant-leader ensure that every view is heard?
2. How can communication within an organization be effective, especially during periods of uncertainty, and what is the most successful way to nullify the impact of the rumormonger?

3. How can quieter, thoughtful colleagues be encouraged to express their views?

Emerging Strategy

There will be times when plans made to secure a major advantage prove to be inadequate, and, rather than securing an advantage, they actually lead to the organization suffering a loss. There can be many reasons for this. Sometimes the full scope of the venture being undertaken could not have been known in advance and the inadequacy of the plans only become apparent at a later date. At other times the reason for failure is due to another person or organization possessing an advantage that could not have been foreseen. However, there are times when the failure occurs because of a deficiency within the servant-leader's own organization.

It may be that the person given the responsibility for making the plans was insufficiently prepared or unsuitable for the task or eventual circumstances.

When the loss is substantial and unexpected, and the servant-leader is made aware that the loss came as a result of someone within the organization, the servant-leader may feel dispirited and, in extreme cases, may even question the worthwhileness of the overall mission of the organization.

At this point, someone who has the ear and confidence of the servant-leader must speak positively and encourage the servant-leader to face the challenges that these new circumstances bring. The challenges are many and include preparing new strategies to meet the new circumstances, or revising existing strategies to ensure that the organization and its people are equipped to meet the challenge of what needs to be achieved.

The person who caused the failure must also be dealt with appropriately and speedily. Where the individual acted innocently, but naïvely, one course of action is appropriate; in other circumstances a different course of action may be needed.

The servant-leader must decide whether the original objectives were realistic, even if the strategies to obtain them were deficient. If the servant-leader is confident that the objectives can be achieved, he or she should take personal responsibility for leading the revised plans. The servant-leader should be personally associated with success or failure (making sure that success is the likely outcome, of course), and by so doing the servant-leader will inspire the followers in the organization and help everyone to overcome the sense of failure that may have permeated the organization. As the servant-leader "goes into battle," he or she should ensure that sufficient and proper resources are given to the venture and that a full complement of other leaders is committed to the venture. Victory can never be guaranteed, but such commitment is rarely wasted.

A servant-leader should not pursue every business opportunity that presents itself. There is a need to place all opportunities in order of priority and to have the courage to recognize and dispense with those activities that are meaningless. Otherwise, it is far too easy for the servant-leader's time to become consumed with activities that are of little, or perhaps even no, worth to the aims of the organization. Some leaders are constantly busy, and some might even think that busying oneself in the pursuit of activity is worthwhile, but the wise servant-leader is the one who is prepared to identify certain activities as meaningless. Meaningless activities should seldom be performed.

Servant-leaders will pay careful attention to the strengths of their organization and be aware of its potential and actual weaknesses. A servant-leader knows that to fail to take action to remedy the weaknesses within the organization is to invite other people—likely one's competitors—to take advantage of the weaknesses and harm the organization's reputation and business.

If the organization is being attacked, it is understandable if servant-leaders wish to spend some time mourning the fact, but they realize that mourning is of no utility in fending off the challenge. Occasionally, the challenges may be extremely difficult to overcome and it is for this reason that servant-leaders understand that to identify their own weaknesses early and eliminate those weaknesses is essential: Prevention is clearly a state to be preferred.

REFERENCES 20–22

Questions

1. What should a servant-leader do when someone in the organization fails? What are the differences between failure that results from an "honest" attempt and failure that was caused by a poorly prepared team?
2. What particular responsibilities does the senior servant-leader have when something goes badly wrong? What remedies are available?
3. How does a servant-leader differentiate between major opportunities when they present themselves and other opportunities that will only result in the organization losing some reserves of energy?
4. What must a servant-leader do to ensure that his or her organization is equipped properly to handle any challenges to its future?

Choosing Tactics

Servant-leaders will not enter into some form of partnership or pact with another organization, or with other individual leaders, until they are content that the motives of the other party are genuine and satisfy the best interests of all concerned.

Many people, and their organizations, will seek to be associated with a servant-leader who is seen to be successful, especially if they believe that an alliance with the organization and its people will protect them from other rival organizations. Servant-leaders proceed with caution in these circumstances, for many leaders have discovered that people are not always what they make themselves out to be. They may misrepresent themselves in crucial areas.

However, once an agreement has been made, the honorable servant-leader will insist on meeting the commitments made in the agreement, and will feel that the spirit of the agreement has been broken if later discovering that certain facts were misrepresented. The servant-leader knows that it is far better to take time, in the exploratory and planning stages of a potential alliance, to find out as much as possible about the real reasons for the proposed alliance.

If disagreements arise over the creation of policy, or over the implementation of such policies, servant-leaders who adhere to differing views should bring the matter before the next level of leader. The different views should be handled with a genuine spirit of inquiry and should not be taken as a personal battle between two or more factions within the organization. The differing views should be aired clearly, without fear of rancor or ridicule, and the parties should be encouraged to reflect on each other's views.

Once there has been full consideration of the various issues—and the presentation and the consideration of the views should be done as speedily as possible—the senior servant-leader will arrive at a decision. This decision will be explained in detail and then communicated to all other interested persons as soon as possible. Where the decision represents a new policy, or a new interpretation of an existing policy, the people who brought the issue to the more senior leader will accept the decision and ensure that all their subsequent actions and motives are seen to be consistent with that decision.

REFERENCES 23–24

Questions

1. What criteria should a servant-leader employ to determine whether a potential ally should be allowed to join or partner the organization?
2. If an honest evaluation and determination of different policy options is to be commended, how can this become standard practice in an organization? And how can people genuinely commit themselves to the implementation and promulgation of the chosen course of action when they did not support the original concept?

Change and Challenge

Servant-leaders know that there may come a time when their authority is challenged, and the challenge may be made in front of others. The challenge has to be dealt with quickly and effectively. The servant-leader should ascertain the names of those making the challenge, others associating themselves with the challenge, and the overt and covert reasons for the challenge.

The reasons are often associated with three factors:

1. Those making the challenge have become arrogant and believe that their own position and contributions are far more exalted than others consider them to be.
2. They may think that senior leaders have distanced themselves from the conditions being experienced by others in the organization, and the justification for such a separation is difficult to sustain.
3. The enterprise as a whole could be experiencing harsh or changing circumstances and people want to express annoyance and frustration with the changing circumstances.

Such open, and in some cases hostile, challenge has to be dealt with swiftly. It has to be shown that the servant-leader is the person with the ultimate responsibility for leadership, although there are times when the servant-leader can use the challenge as an opportunity to explain once more the reasons for a particular course of action.

Servant-leaders realize that challenges of this nature may not have been mounted with pure motives and therefore leaders must act decisively. However, there are two major benefits arising from such challenges:

1. It provides a servant-leader with an opportunity to demonstrate that he or she exercises overall leadership, and in the process the challenge can be used to strengthen the approach taken by the leader.
2. It enables servant-leaders to spend time explaining to those who genuinely misunderstand the issues, or understand the

issues but question the key decisions that have been taken, the reasons for the course of action and how alternative courses of action were considered and dismissed.

Although the points raised may have been dismissed, sensible servant-leaders will ponder the issues at some length, as some points may have a grain of truth in them even though they were raised with incorrect motives. The circumstances described in this principle are not similar to those times when there is an opportunity for all decisions to be considered by everyone and where servant-leaders positively welcome different views and the discussion of alternative courses of action. A servant-leader is skilled in differentiating between the genuine and the manipulative.

The majority of leaders are happy to announce good and welcome news to their people, but one of the important tasks of a servant-leader is to be prepared to state unpleasant truths about performance. A servant-leader will always bear in mind the purpose of the organization, its values and principles, the role of the people and ensure, from time to time, that there is a fundamental review of these matters.

This ensures that the organization does not unintentionally stray from the path it set itself. To stray from the path intentionally is one thing, but to stray from the path unwittingly may court disaster. The servant-leader will take stock of the situation and, where there is a deviation between what was intended and what has occurred, will bring these facts to the attention of all concerned and ensure that remedial action is taken at once. The servant-leader may need to spell out potential difficulties in clear terms. There are times when such interventions should be accompanied by dramatic actions, or the use of imaginative metaphors, to ensure that the seriousness of the issue is understood.

REFERENCES 25–26

Questions

1. There is a fine line to be drawn between encouraging a genuine questioning of decisions that arises from an open style of leadership and the unhelpful questioning of leader-

ship decisions. How does a servant-leader tread this fine
line?

2. How should a servant-leader deal with such a challenge to
his or her authority and also what lessons can the servant-
leader learn from this experience?

3. Why is it important for a servant-leader to be willing to
announce good and bad news and to ensure that there are
regular reviews of whether the organization is committed
to its original foundational values and policies?

Discipline and Accountability

Wise servant-leaders take time at regular intervals to ensure
that individual actions are in keeping with the aims and values of
the organization. An organization should set out the nature of its
activities and the way in which those activities are to be conducted.
Where there is a difference between the aims and values of the
organization and the practice of an individual, action can be taken
to remedy the situation. Where small deviations are allowed to
continue unquestioned and uncorrected, they may grow in size and
become large deviations. Large deviations between theory and
practice are likely to result in long-term, adverse consequences for
the organization. Ensuring that practice is being undertaken cor-
rectly should be valued in the organization, as it often saves considerable pain at a later date.

A servant-leader carries a heavy responsibility particularly
when the people being led have given the leader their full alle-
giance. The worst thing a leader can do is to misuse that trust. A
servant-leader understands that he or she is accountable to those
being led. The commitment of people is never to be taken for
granted; where commitment is taken for granted it is often lost.
The servant-leader should be prepared to explain their leadership
style, the values that are being pursued, the high points and the difficult low points for the organization, the challenges that have been
met, and the commitment shown by the servant-leader to the needs
of the organization. The servant-leader who has generated trust,
based on a full account of past actions, is far more likely to receive

approval for future plans, especially where the full details of future plans are unavailable. The servant-leader who shows that he or she is motivated entirely by the mission of the organization and its people will be trusted to a far greater extent than other types of leader.

Regrettably, there are times when the behavior and perform-ance of certain leaders is so unacceptable that they have to be excluded from any further involvement with the organization. They are unsuitable for any further training, and to continue their association with the organization would be an unhealthy example to others. Action should be undertaken quickly and, although regrettable, serves as an example.

On other occasions, directions issued by a servant-leader may not have been followed fully by others. When this is a result of carelessness or lack of attention, rather than a result of changing circumstances where it was appropriate to use initiative and change the plan, errors should be identified and action taken to rectify matters.

References 27–31

Questions

1. What part does discipline have to play in leadership and why is it essential for a servant-leader to understand the dif-ferences between discipline as a corrective action and learn-ing experience and discipline as a purely punitive measure?
2. How open should a servant-leader be in revealing the true state of affairs of the organization during each stage of a venture, or at regular intervals in the calendar?

Application of Servant-Leadership

Successful servant-leaders realize that their personal effective-ness is linked inextricably to the quality of the other leaders who sup-port them. Effective leadership can only be achieved when there are other leaders of sufficient quality and loyalty. These other servant-leaders are people who understand the overall needs of the business and are clear about what the organization must do to succeed. They are also prepared to use every legitimate approach to achieve their aims, and they demonstrate undivided loyalty to their leader.

The servant-leader is always aware that there are others in the organization, often people who are far more junior in age and status, who may have a greater insight into key issues, and a greater understanding of what needs to be done. Wisdom, insight, and understanding are not the sole prerogative of those who carry senior roles.

Servant-leaders ensure that active procedures exist to provide opportunities for all people, irrespective of age and status, to suggest ways in which matters should be taken forward. Servant-leaders ensure that younger people, who possess talent and different ways of addressing issues, are heard and prosper. Many an organization has experienced difficult times when it has allowed only those with an acknowledged seniority to decide future courses of action. In so doing it has precluded young people, especially those who see new and exciting opportunities, from contributing to the decision-making process or from actually leading a key initiative.

The servant-leader pays particular regard to the various needs of the people being led and ensures that their needs are met. The servant-leader realizes that needs differ with different people and that, over time, an individual's needs may differ greatly. The servant-leader will exercise care and have the interests of those being led close to his or her heart. The servant-leader also puts in place special provisions for those times when one of the people being led has to pay special attention to needs within the family, such as raising children.

Newly appointed servant-leaders pay considerable attention to the application of their leadership, as inappropriate actions send out unfortunate messages. A wise servant-leader, on entering an organization for the first time, meets with the people and listens to their views about the needs of the organization and then asks for advice from other servant-leaders within the organization. Where older and more experienced leaders suggest one form of leadership and younger, and perhaps more impatient, leaders suggest another style, the new leader should consider this advice carefully and only choose a particular approach after much thought.

Some leaders have rushed into this decision, or have thought that the advice from one group would automatically be better than the advice of another group, and as a result have made errors of judgment and introduced inappropriate practices. This results in their leadership effectiveness being harmed.

Where inappropriate practices have been introduced, and then seen to be an error, the servant-leader will be humble enough to admit that an error has been made and will amend the practices immediately. Even if some people keep a record of the error in their minds, it is far better to change, and to be remembered for an earlier error, than to continue with practices that are out of keeping with the needs of the organization.

Servant-leaders ensure that the leadership given is highly visible, that communications are clear and frequent, and that those being led are in no doubt about the direction being given. The two overriding challenges for the servant-leader are to give clear direction and to be visible. Servant-leaders need to be strong. They should not be sentimental in their decision making; otherwise, some unprincipled people may seek to take advantage of them. The attitude of the servant-leader is to care continually for the interests of the people being led *and* for their own position.

Some leaders believe that an autocratic style of leadership is more associated with determination and power, but that is not the case with a servant-leader. It is much better to practice leadership that everyone in the organization believes to be fair and that will encourage everyone to give their best.

REFERENCES 32–37

Questions

1. Why is it important for a servant-leader to introduce leadership practices in keeping with the culture of the organization and the demands being faced by the enterprise? Are there times when these two criteria (culture and demands) are in conflict?

2. Why is it that some people make good lieutenants but poor captains and some people make good captains but poor lieutenants?

3. What mechanisms can be put in place to ensure that the knowledge, experience, and ideas of all people can be used effectively?

4. Why is it important to make special provision for the personal and family needs of those being led?

Stewardship and Personal Probity

Most organizations possess rules and regulations, codes of conduct, standing instructions, ways in which activities should be undertaken, and other guidance documents. These are made explicit to assist each individual, and servant-leaders ensure that everyone understands that freedom to experiment and innovation have to stand alongside necessary regulations. Some people prefer to observe regulations in theory but not in practice, and this can result in unfortunate consequences for the individuals and the organization.

When engaging in a major piece of work, wise servant-leaders ensure that clear approval has been obtained for the work they are about to undertake. Otherwise, there may be those, including people who have been given the job of assessing the probity of all actions, who will question the legitimacy of the work and the individuals performing it. It is insufficient to demonstrate that the work is beneficial if, in fact, those in authority have not approved the work.

Authority usually emanates from within the organization, but there are circumstances when the servant-leader will be engaged in activities for another body where the question of authority has not been clarified. The servant-leader should ensure that the full extent of accountabilities has been clarified and that authority to undertake those tasks has been fully delegated. At other times, specific tasks may emerge within one's own organization where it is essential to understand the full scope of one's mandate and that those holding greater authority than the servant-leader fully support the proposed course of action and will support the leader if there are troubled waters to be navigated.

There may be an occasion when a person will act dishonorably on the basis of his or her close association with the senior leader. The close associate may even issue instructions to other leaders using papers that give the impression that it is the senior leader who is issuing the instruction. If someone considers the instructions to be unusual, from a servant-leader they know so well, they should be encouraged to question the authenticity of those instructions. They should feel able to raise questions without any fear of punitive action.

References 38–41

Questions

1. Why has the term *doing things by the book* almost become a pejorative term?
2. How is it possible to ensure that adhering to rules governing the conduct of business does not inhibit someone from using initiative and acting intuitively?
3. Why is it essential for a servant-leader to be clear about the task to be performed and the authority given to him or her to accomplish the task?

Learning

Servant-leaders ensure that they associate themselves with men and women of learning on a regular basis and that the learning is used within their organizations. They will also make opportunities to learn from one another. It is an unwise person who finds that he or she is too busy to take part in learning events.

A servant-leader understands that it is possible to learn from success and failure. When a person experiences failure there are two possible responses:

1. The person, unwisely, will act as if nothing happened and the failure is never referred to or, worse still, there is an attempt to represent the failure as some kind of victory.
2. Or the person, sensibly, will use the failure as a positive means of learning within the organization and will encourage a full and frank discussion of the events that led to the defeat.

Through this reflection valuable lessons may be learned.

There are times when a servant-leader has to question the actions of another leader, possibly in front of other leaders, where the servant-leader believes that an intended or actual course of action is wrong. This is a courageous act, as it may incur the disapproval of one's leadership colleagues, but it should be undertaken when the principles are important and *no other course of action is available*. The servant-leader will be courageous enough to challenge the acts of another, and the optimal organization is one where others commend such action.

If the servant-leader is incorrect in the challenge, then he or she should be sufficiently humble to withdraw the remarks. Where the servant-leader is correct in the challenge, the other leaders should be grateful for such a courageous and helpful challenge and change their intended course of action.

REFERENCES 42–44

Questions

1. What benefits accrue to a servant-leader who is committed to regular formal and informal learning sessions?
2. Facing up to failure and reflecting on the experience are essential for a servant-leader. Why is this the case?
3. What factors should a servant-leader bear in mind before choosing to confront a fellow leader in front of other colleagues?

Commitment, Communication, and Feedback

When the servant-leader is inexperienced, it is the duty of those who are older and wiser to support him or her. They recognize the role of the servant-leader, but, being aware of the leader's inexperience and the possibility that the leader may make errors of judgment, the older and wiser people ensure that there is a wall of protection around the servant-leader.

Servant-leaders are willing to give generously to the work of the organization. In rare circumstances, some may even give financial support, but in all cases servant-leaders are willing to give generously in kind, especially of their talents and time. Where servant-leaders give generously, their people celebrate the willing response of their leaders and their wholehearted commitment. They, in turn, will often be inspired to give their utmost for the future prosperity of the organization.

A servant-leader, especially when working in an organization opposed to the principles of servant-leadership, may experience loneliness and a feeling of isolation. The servant-leader carries heavy responsibilities that, at times, may feel like challenges that cannot be overcome. The servant-leader needs to have associates who are willing to encourage him or her and praise the work that is being undertaken: A servant-leader needs to have positive feedback as much as those who are being led.

Those offering praise and support must ensure that their own attitudes are free of ulterior motives and that they are not offering praise and support to advance their own position. Praise for the servant-leader should come from a mature person. This act of support is extremely important.

Some immature leaders believe, or act as if they believe, that when an important decision has been made, one that affects all within the organization, it is adequate to write down the decision, as some form of policy or communiqué, and issue it to all concerned. These immature leaders appear to believe that the document will be read by all, understood, agreed upon, that the decisions will be implemented immediately, and that practices and behaviors, often practices and behaviors that have been present for decades, will be altered immediately or as soon as possible. Such leaders are misled in their thinking and are rarely servant-leaders.

When an important decision has been made, a servant-leader realizes that it is necessary for it to be recorded and for those who made the decision to visit various parts of the organization to communicate the decision, to discuss its implications, and to explain how past practices should be amended.

The next step should be for other servant-leaders, who are sufficiently senior and respected, to spend considerable time showing people how things should be undertaken following the changes. Through the example of the servant-leaders, new behaviors should be demonstrated daily and consistently.

Once change has occurred, servant-leaders ensure that all parts of the organization, no matter how small or distant, have been visited and that there has been sufficient opportunity to explain the changes and ensure that new practices have been implemented willingly.

REFERENCES 45–47

Questions

1. Is it expecting too much for
   - older and wiser people to support a new and inexperienced servant-leader?
   - servant-leaders to give generously (mainly of their time and talents) to the organization?
2. How can a servant-leader know that the feedback and support received from those being led is genuine?
3. What are the principal stages a servant-leader should follow to implement successfully a key policy decision throughout the organization?

The Appointment of Servant-Leaders and the Question of Succession

Transparency

The choice of a new servant-leader, especially where it involves the successor to a highly respected and successful former servant-leader, is an extremely important activity within the organization. It is treated with great care, and attention is paid to the systems employed to choose the successor. The process should be transparent, so that no one can complain about favoritism or nepotism and so that the process will be open to all those who consider themselves as potential successors. The two principles of transparency and openness do much to reduce possible resentment against the person eventually appointed. A third principle will also be observed: Objective criteria should be established to select the successor and the criteria should be communicated to all interested parties.

There are occasions when it is beneficial for the servant-leader, who is stepping down, to be a part of the selection process, especially where the departing servant-leader is highly regarded. In this way the passing of the leadership role will be smoother and the highly desirable attributes of the former servant-leader can be more easily seen as existing or potential attributes within the new servant-leader.

Once the decision concerning the new servant-leader has been made, all other leaders will acknowledge the new leader and ensure that there is no criticism in public of the choice. If there is any dissent concerning the decision, this should not be expressed, as it can easily cause damage to the reputation of an organization.

REFERENCE 48

Questions

1. What is the best recruitment and selection process you have experienced or observed being used in the choice of a new servant-leader?
2. What is the most appropriate way for a new servant-leader to be welcomed into an organization?

Leading during the Interregnum

A servant-leader will know when the time has come to lay down the responsibilities of leadership and pass them on to someone else. It may be that the servant-leader has reached an age where it is wise to retire, or the leader may have reached a career stage where it is clear that he or she has little more to offer the organization. At this time, the servant-leader will act positively by agreeing that an announcement be made and ensuring that a relatively short gap exists between the announcement of a change and its implementation. Otherwise, there will be an unacceptable period of uncertainty during which some people may jostle for position and power rather than deliver the needs of the organization.

The period between the departure of a servant-leader and the appointment of a new leader can be a difficult time for an organization. Because of the authority and reputation of the retiring leader some conflict may have lain dormant in the organization, but during a period of transfer to a new leader there may be occasions when this conflict rises to the surface.

The former and new servant-leader need to be aware of the possibility of such conflict, and any disruptive people will need to be challenged concerning their behavior. This challenge may be best delivered by the former servant-leader, as he or she is more likely to know the full scope of the issues.

A retiring servant-leader will remind those who continue to run the organization of the key principles and values that earned the organization its reputation and will encourage the next generation of servant-leaders to maintain these principles and values.

The next generation of servant-leaders will need to be strong; they will ensure that the transition is handled smoothly and that the interests of those they lead receive appropriate attention. Often, it is timely for the retiring servant-leader, when recalling the great successes of the organization and the principles upon which those triumphs were secured, to present a challenge concerning the next generation's role in future success.

REFERENCES 49–50

Questions

1. What measures should be put in place to ensure that the handover from one servant-leader to another is as smooth and problem-free as possible?
2. Why do some leaders wait too long before "hanging up their boots" and therefore leave the organization without as much acclaim as if they had departed some years or months previously?
3. Does a former servant-leader have any role to play in the organization once he or she has handed over the reins? If so, what should that role be?

Experiencing Feelings of Barrenness

In organizations hostile to the principles of servant-leadership, some individual servant-leaders may experience a stage in their careers that is barren, a desert time rather than a fertile period, when they believe that they have been cast aside and will never again take the reins of a department or unit. This is an experience common to many leaders. It can arise because of a family issue, or a current senior leader taking a dislike to a previous leader (or to someone associated with a previous leader), or because of being associated with an initiative that is no longer in favor, or even because of one's chosen leadership style.

A servant-leader experiencing such barren times should not lose heart but take the barren period as an opportunity for reflection, a time to strengthen resolve, and he or she must retain belief that a new area of activity will present itself in due course. The servant-leader will remain positive, prepare to recommence leadership when an opportunity arrives, and accept the challenge of leadership in new arenas.

There are times when those who caused the servant-leader to enter a barren period will realize that new circumstances being faced by their organization require that the former servant-leader return to a key leadership role with them. Ironically, it is only by the return of the former servant-leader that the organization will feel confident in overcoming the new challenges being faced. In such circumstances the servant-leader will act cautiously, as it may be expediency alone that has generated the request for a return to the former role. If the servant-leader decides to return, then it will be undertaken with great attention to detail and there will be explicit conditions concerning the nature of the return and the responsibilities to be undertaken. A servant-leader returning to a prominent position resists any urge for retribution against those who acted against him or her.

REFERENCE 51

Questions

1. How can a servant-leader, who is clearly out of favor, turn this period to his or her advantage by using it as a time of refreshing?
2. How does a deposed servant-leader retain dignity and why should he or she refrain from any attempt at retribution?

Dealing with "New Brooms" (Who Are Not Servant-Leaders)

Change for change's sake, especially the desire to experiment with alternative systems, is not always a good thing. Many organizations, with a record of success and previous procedures that appeared eminently sensible, have experienced times when dissatisfaction arose and they believed that things would be much better if only a new leader were appointed. They believed the new leader would introduce new systems and methods and their organization would imitate the way another enterprise organized itself.

Sometimes the pressure for change can be substantial, and changes are forced upon one and all. At first the changes have the appearance of improving all facets of life for the people in the organization, and there is a sense that the new leader is the best leader that ever led the organization: "There is no one like him in this or any other similar organization." But, over time, another side of the leader is seen that is totally unsatisfactory and not in the best interests of the people or the organization.

If this deterioration happens, those who forced through the changes become dissatisfied with the changes they supported and helped implement. Before long, plans are formulated to remove the leader from the post and to replace him or her with someone who is far closer to the previous arrangements, with someone who will ensure that the old values of the organization are reinstated and adhered to firmly.

This becomes a great lesson to all and should remind everyone that to rush into a new set of arrangements, especially ones that overturn the ways in which things have been done for generations, can be fraught with danger. The appointment of a new leader has to be treated carefully, as there are far too many examples of appointments being nigh on disastrous for the reputation of the organization. Fortunately, there are those who learn from such dire experiences and who ensure that their subsequent leader is chosen diligently, with the closest attention being paid to the attributes required for the post and the greatest care given to choosing the most able person for the post. It might even lead some of them to consider the advantages of appointing servant-leaders.

REFERENCE 52

Questions

1. There are times when a new leader can transform an organization and there are times when a new leader fails spectacularly. From your experience, are there general principles to follow in making such appointments?
2. Does the phrase "change for change's sake" suggest a common problem in the appointment of such leaders?
3. Why is it that some organizations can be "taken in" by the charms of some leaders and forget that the organization's reputation was built on more solid foundations?

Succession Planning

Succession from one servant-leader to another will be meticulously planned and in many situations may involve the transfer of authority to someone within the organization who has been earmarked to assume leadership at the appropriate time.

The departing servant-leader will play a major role in ensuring that the transfer of power is smooth and effective. Also, there is a need for the new leader to be clear about the major tasks that have to be tackled and to make extensive preparations for the transfer of leadership responsibilities.

The former leader will ensure that the new leader is briefed fully on the issues concerning work to be accomplished, recognize the potential in the next generation of leadership to fulfill what is required, understand that the passing of responsibility from one generation to another is highly desirable, explain to the new leader the provisions and facilities that are at his or her disposal and give access to them immediately. The new servant-leader will be advised to be courageous, to attend to the work of the organization, to be wholehearted, and to possess a positive and willing attitude. The skills of those working with the new servant-leader should also be explained and then the new leader must be wished every success. The final act of the former leader should be to invite all other, more junior, leaders in the organization to support the new leader in the venture and to do their utmost to guarantee success for all concerned.

The new leader should accept the counsel of the former servant-leader.

When the trustees or directors of an organization meet to appoint a chief leader, a person they are willing to represent them in all activities, they must ensure that there is no difference between what they *say* they want in their chief leader and what they actually want. They should be prepared to accept advice from those better placed to help in such decisions and pay careful attention to the achievements of the organization in more recent times.

References 53–54

Questions

1. Does a system of succession planning ensure the continued success of the organization or does it limit the choice of new leaders to an existing complement of leaders?
2. What key role can the departing servant-leader play in ensuring that there is a smooth transition to the new servant-leader?
3. How can an organization ensure that the qualities they have specified for a new servant-leader are those that will best serve the organization?

Servant-Leadership and Management

Structure

A servant-leader will ensure that appropriate structures exist throughout the organization. Where the servant-leader is not the most appropriate person to make such organizational arrangements then he or she will ensure that someone is appointed, as a senior deputy, to put such arrangements in place. Many organizations have seen plans come to nought as a result of poor, or even nonexistent, organizational arrangements. Consequently, the servant-leader highly values the skills of someone gifted in making such arrangements.

Each part of the organization should have a servant-leader, and there should be no confusion concerning the chain of command, as the absence of such clarity can have unfortunate consequences. Through effective organizational settings, the decisions of a servant-leader can be communicated to all parts of the organization, implemented consistently, and the results of the actions communicated in return to the servant-leaders.

The persons appointed to servant-leadership roles should be suited to the task set them. Some servant-leaders will be better suited to lead certain groups of people and others will be better suited to lead other groups. It is important for the overall servant-leader to recognize the relative strengths and suitability of the leadership team.

Since there are many times when the organizational arrangements will be imperfect, a servant-leader will make use of the resources available and not complain that exact arrangements and people have failed to materialize. Above all, the overall servant-leader will do his or her utmost to provide those servant-leaders, in charge of newly formed divisions, with the resources needed to do their jobs well.

REFERENCE 55

Questions

1. How important a role does a co-leader or deputy leader have to play in the success of the organization?
2. Is the notion of a "chain of command" old-fashioned or is it an essential component for all types of organizations?
3. Why is it unfair to ask someone to lead a division and then deprive them of the resources to carry out their responsibilities? Can you explain why some organizations do this to their leaders?

Roles

In addition to the servant-leadership roles exercised by those in charge of people engaged in operational matters, there is a need to appoint servant-leaders who will be responsible for the care of money and the care of all other resources on behalf of the organization.

Many other roles and responsibilities have to be undertaken on behalf of the overall servant-leader. Other servant-leaders need to be gathered together, and the overall objectives, and what is required of each other leader, must be explained clearly. Some servant-leaders will concern themselves with future projects, others will maintain the present arrangements to ensure success throughout the organization, and still others will work closely with the senior leadership for encouragement and support in the various aspects of running a large enterprise.

References 56–57

Questions

1. Why is it there a temptation for some leaders engaged in operational activities to consider themselves more important than those leaders engaged in support or functional activities?
2. What can be done to ensure that everyone understands the role they have to play and how it complements the role undertaken by other servant-leaders?

Management

Servant-leaders will ensure that throughout the organization there are networks of managers who are experienced, possess sound judgment, and who are committed to the organization and its aims. Without such managers an organization is unlikely to run successfully. Where managers are seen to perform their duties conscientiously, and demonstrate loyalty, their efforts should be rewarded through granting either greater responsibilities or other suitable rewards.

One key way by which the performance of a manager should be judged is on how employees reporting to him or her are treated. A servant-leader will ensure that all persons in the organization are treated honorably and that their individual dignity is respected.

Servant-leaders will be aware that, very occasionally, managers might take advantage of the freedom given to them. When the leader is away, attending to other matters, for example, these managers will mismanage the affairs of the organization and may even abuse their position. The servant-leader will ensure that the performance of such managers is checked—without necessarily giving due notice of such an examination—and take action if appropriate. A manager acting in such an inappropriate style may be "offered the opportunity" to undertake nonmanagerial work.

When a person has been given a position of authority, a great deal will be expected of that person, far more than will be expected of a person who has not been entrusted with much responsibility.

If a servant-leader becomes aware that a manager is acting dishonorably, or if questions are raised concerning the manager's capability or conduct, then the servant-leader will speak to the manager, make that person aware of the allegations or concerns, and give the manager an opportunity to respond. If the allegations or concerns are found to be true, then the servant-leader will take appropriate action, which could include the manager losing his or her position. However, the servant-leader will be aware that many people respond well to being given a second chance—an opportunity to make amends for previous unacceptable actions. The servant-leader welcomes and celebrates such a positive outcome.

Servant-leaders realize that there are times when a second chance brings about a transformation in the behavior of an individual and will do everything in their power to allow that to happen. The servant-leader also takes into account the fundamental question of trust. The general principle appears to be that a person who can be trusted with little can also be trusted with much; when a person cannot be trusted with little, he or she is unlikely to be trustworthy with greater amounts of responsibility. This is a difficult area for the servant-leader to judge.

REFERENCES 58–59

Questions

1. Can leadership exist without management and can management exist without leadership? Are the two concepts (leadership and management) quite separate or are they inseparable twins?
2. How crucial is mutual respect to the effectiveness of the organization?
3. What practical and effective actions will a servant-leader take with a manager who has abused the responsibility and authority given to him or her?

Servant-Leadership and Followers

Surviving through Difficult Times

Servant-leaders appreciate that a time may come when they are asked to provide leadership to a group of followers who are not the most impressive of people. As a result of recent experiences, these followers may be exhibiting signs of distress, or they may have substantial financial problems, or they may be a gathering of followers who, for whatever reason, have allowed themselves to become discontent with what life and, more importantly, with what the organization has to offer them. Such circumstances are a challenge for the servant-leader and will certainly test the leader's mettle.

The servant-leader will rise to the challenge and tackle each of the followers' inhibitions. Those who are distressed will be given a reason for optimism; those who have financial problems will be given help to resolve their problems; and those who are discontent will be helped to overcome their negative positions and shown attitudes that are necessary for them and the organization to prosper. Most followers respond positively and are grateful for the opportunities given to them. In circumstances where the followers do not respond, they will be asked to leave the organization and others will be given the opportunities they have squandered.

Servant-leaders may experience a time when their leadership is questioned by followers. This is particularly true when the servant-leader and followers have experienced a major disappointment or a series of disappointments. The servant-leader will remain positive and if necessary find someone to speak to who will assist in focusing on the tasks at hand. The servant-leader will act positively and show, as quickly as possible, the followers that he or she possesses plans to recover the ground that has been lost.

The plans will be put into action as soon as possible and the best followers will be utilized in the actions to ensure that success is the result of the new campaign. Where other followers are willing, but unable, to help—this may be as a result of their stress or physical condition—then they should be assigned other responsibilities to support the efforts of those taking the main actions.

When the plans have been achieved, and the organization has prospered, all those who took part in the actions, plus those who were genuinely unable to take part, should benefit to the same extent from the rewards of the success.

Sometimes, followers appear fickle and may wish to abandon the principles and values that built the reputation of the organization. In such ways, followers demonstrate that they are not leaders, and leaderless followers often encounter disaster.

REFERENCES 60–62

Questions

1. Is it an opportunity or a threat to the career of the servant-leader to be asked to lead a group of people who, quite frankly, appear to be a hopeless case?
2. Does the experience of adversity strengthen a servant-leader in the medium to long term or do a series of adversities weaken the servant-leader?
3. How does a servant-leader counter fickleness among some followers?

Exercising Sound Judgement

An experienced servant-leader will acknowledge that the success of his or her leadership is directly related to the strength and ability of the followers. No servant-leader can achieve everything that is necessary for the success of the organization on their own, and the quality of the followers is a critical factor in success or failure. Where followers are experienced and can be trusted to deliver in their area of activity, then the servant-leader is more likely to be successful.

When a servant-leader establishes a reputation for being successful and communicates a sense of purpose, a number of potential followers will emerge who wish to be associated with the servant-leader and future successes. The servant-leader, in most cases, will welcome such new followers, assign them meaningful work, and expect them to deliver significant results. The fact that the new followers are more interested in success than in most other issues can be an asset as long as the servant-leader uses this wisely and channels the followers' efforts in the right direction.

A servant-leader may have a band of dedicated followers, they may even have worked closely with the leader over a long period of time, sharing times of danger and challenge, or times when they needed the support of one another, but the servant-leader will be aware that the loyalty of the closest of followers must never be taken for granted. The servant-leader will pay attention to the needs of the followers for status, finance, and recognition. If attention is not paid to these issues, the result can be disloyalty by the person once considered a colleague and friend. The servant-leader will ensure that where such challenges arise they must not be insurmountable; they must be overcome without undue damage to the servant-leader, the follower, and the organization.

Servant-leaders will be concerned if other leaders (who are not servant-leaders) in the organization set out to choose a team of close followers who are somewhat reckless in that they appear not to care about the interests of anyone other than themselves, and adventurous in that they appear to suspend sound judgment in preference for the thrill of being engaged in something considered daring. Such arrangements usually result in poor consequences. Those who observe such daring disregard in the appointment of the leader's close followers should present their concerns and consider carefully whether they should attempt to thwart the plans.

REFERENCES 63–66

Questions

1. Is it possible to assess the judgment of a servant-leader by the company he or she keeps?
2. Can leading a successful organization be as difficult as leading one in decline?
3. To what extent does a servant-leader owe his or her success to the contribution of key followers and how should this contribution be recognized fully?

Contribution of Followers

As the success of a servant-leader increases, he or she may get more and more influential and, as a result of this growth in authority, incur the envy of powerful leaders in other organizations who see a newly influential leader as a threat to their position. The other leaders may even set out to harm the reputation, status, and position of the newly arrived leader. Followers have a crucial role to play in such circumstances.

It is their responsibility to protect their servant-leader, to work closely with him or her to fend off the attacks of others and to create a means of escape (should one be needed) to ensure the well-being of the servant-leader. At other times the followers should take responsibility for introducing their servant-leader to new opportunities for him or her and the organization. The servant-leader needs to be supported by followers when a role is being established within wider communities. In this way there will be a strengthening of the whole organization and a greater security for all concerned.

Followers will commit themselves to serving the interests of the servant-leader, since following declared policies and recognizing the servant-leader's authority is in the interests of all concerned. Followers will recognize that servant-leaders undertake a difficult role, since they keep watch over all aspects of the organization, seek to meet the needs of followers, and often have to give an account of their actions to a higher authority. Followers will seek to work for the servant-leader in a manner that makes it easier, rather than harder, for the leader to undertake his or her responsibilities. If at all possible the leadership role should be a pleasant role to occupy; when the servant-leader is content it is to the advantage of all concerned.

Followers remember with affection various servant-leaders who taught them through example, who showed them the direction to be taken, and who helped them develop as individuals. The manner in which servant-leaders conduct themselves will be an example. There are other occasions when another leader may have acted dishonorably; in these cases the follower will take the behavior of the leader as a poor example and be grateful for the good example of their servant-leader.

References 67–69

Questions

1. What practical steps can followers take to protect a servant-leader from envious competitors and rivals?
2. What can followers do to make leadership a joy for the servant-leader?
3. How should the example of servant-leaders and leadership in general be celebrated in the organization?

When Leadership Goes Wrong*

Straightforward Error

When a servant-leader commits a serious error unintentionally, it should be acknowledged clearly that an error has been committed. The servant-leader's act of omission or commission should not be covered up, and when the leader becomes aware of the errors he or she should approach those more senior in the organization and explain the nature of the errors.

There are times when errors committed by servant-leaders are a result of lack of knowledge and/or experience. Where this is the case, servant-leaders should be given the opportunity to identify their errors and receive "forgiveness" (if this is relevant). In this way it is likely that servant-leaders will become better leaders as a result of their experience. To remove a servant-leader on the basis of one error, an error probably made as the result of lack of knowledge and/or experience, is both unfair and a waste of useful talent.

When leaders commit wrong actions, one reason for their behavior can be a lack of humility. When leaders have little humil-

---

* This section refers more to leadership in general and not to servant-leadership specifically, unless stated.

ity, they become obsessed with their own position and status and are reluctant to consult with those whom they consider to be inferior. Also, they may develop a hard-heartedness toward the needs of others. Servant-leaders, on the other hand, display humility.

As the errors were committed unintentionally, and as the servant-leader has given a full account, there is an obligation to do everything to restore the servant-leader to his or her former position of respect. The actions necessary to redeem the situation should be agreed upon with the servant-leader, a plan agreed upon to ensure that the errors are not repeated, and lessons should be learned for the benefit of the whole organization.

Inexperienced leaders can fall prey to rhetoric from persuasive people that encourages leaders to take inappropriate action. In their enthusiasm to be seen as men and women of action, leaders can be inspired by such rhetoric. When they have an opportunity for cool reflection, they realize that they acted hastily.

Unchecked errors by a leader can harm the remainder of the organization—more junior leaders can become careless and start following practices that are not commendable. In the end, the organization itself becomes affected adversely.

No servant-leader is perfect. Often imperfections reveal the leader's humanity and can become an attractive characteristic.

REFERENCES 70–71, 78–79

Questions

1. When a servant-leader commits a serious error, how should the organization react, and is it possible to turn the event into a learning experience for the remainder of the organization while restoring the reputation of the servant-leader?
2. Does the behavior of a leader have a direct effect, positively or negatively, on the culture of the organization and thereby the actions of everyone else?
3. Are there occasions when a leader, who has committed a serious error intentionally or unintentionally, should be treated harshly as an example to others?

*Limited Corruption**

One of the worst sets of circumstances that a senior leader can face is to be told that widespread corrupt practices exist within the organization. It is even worse when those corrupt practices have been undertaken by those charged with leading the organization honorably. This is an example of bad practice that strikes at the very heart of the faithfulness that should exist between a senior leader and other leaders. When such a breakdown occurs there must be a full examination of the corruption that has been committed, and the leaders involved in malpractices must be encouraged to give a full account of what took place. Then every wrong practice must be terminated and new systems introduced that cannot be ignored or circumvented.

Once the new arrangements have been agreed upon, all those engaged in senior roles in the organization must be summoned to the central location of the organization and given a full account of the misdemeanors that took place, why the regulations of the organization were flaunted, the systems that have been introduced to ensure that such a breach does not occur again, and finally they should be told the behavior and actions that are necessary from them in order to restore the reputation of the organization. The leaders who allowed such malpractices to occur should be dealt with in accordance with their behavior and the damage it caused to the reputation of the organization.

There are substantial consequences for organizations when leaders do not adhere to the principles and best practices associated with sound leadership. The people of the organization are likely to experience hardship as a direct result of the neglect of the leaders. When the leaders have strayed from established practice and committed themselves to foolhardy practices, their people pay the price for their foolishness. The leaders may have enjoyed various short-term benefits as a result of their practices, but they have stored up

---

* In this section, and the next, the term *servant-leadership* has not been used, since one expects that such behavior falls outside the very essence of being a servant-leader.

trouble for themselves and, worse still, for others and for the organization as a whole.

The consequences are regrettable and ones that could have been avoided if only sensible habits had been followed. The result is that the people who trusted their leaders have lost many benefits and may, in time, come under the leadership of another organization, one that does not genuinely have their interests at heart. The benefits that could have accrued to the people are now being realized and enjoyed by other people. All this is because of the negligence of certain leaders.

Leaders carry a heavy responsibility for their own actions and for the actions of those they lead. The rewards of leadership may be potentially large but so are the consequences when leadership is exercised irresponsibly. In such times, leaders can expect to receive punitive recognition for what happened within their area of responsibility.

REFERENCES 72–74

Questions

1. Does the issue of the governance of an organization strike at the very heart of the health of the enterprise and the reputation of its leadership? If that is the case, then why is it that some leaders adopt such a cavalier attitude to these things?
2. Can an organization recover from a position where members of the public consider many of its leaders to be corrupt?
3. What measures should be introduced to prevent widespread bad practice?

Extensive Corruption

It is possible for an entire organization to be corrupt in the way it deals with people and other organizations. The corruption has spread through the enterprise like a cancer and infected each and every part. It seems that there is not a single person in the whole of the organization who deals honestly and attempts to operate under the simple direction of "what is true." When such an organization is discovered, everyone hopes that its leaders will be different, that they will be upright and honorable in their dealings. But the truth is that in some enterprises even the most senior leaders have been corrupted; perhaps it was the leaders who were corrupted first and then they influenced everyone else for the worse. It is possible that the entire leadership has yielded to systems and practices that cannot be justified.

Although leadership is a noble activity and leaders are worthy of the honor given to them, it is a sad fact that some leaders are given to plotting ignoble acts, and their plans include the accomplishment of unacceptable practices at the expense of innocent people. These leaders and their corrupt practices should be exposed. Men and women of courage should not be afraid to speak out to expose corrupt intent. Within all organizations there should be procedures to allow people of honor to expose any corrupt practices being planned or executed by their leaders. The exposure and termination of deplorable leadership acts is of great importance.

Leaders who use their skills and energy to mislead and exploit ordinary people are worthy of the utmost contempt. Leaders should be people who stand for justice, and yet there are some leaders who prefer wrong deeds to good deeds. They exploit their people and treat them with contempt. Some leaders act on the basis of the favors they have received rather than on a correct judgment of what is required to be undertaken. Such leaders are corrupt and contemptible. People who are believers in justice and who possess the necessary power should expose the corrupt practices of these leaders and show that the leaders have distorted what is right for their own selfish gain. Leaders who make judgments on the basis of a bribe should be exposed for what they are—corrupt and unworthy of holding any sort of office.

REFERENCES 75–77

Questions

1. We know that corrupt organizations exist. Why is this the case and what can someone working in them do to expose their wrongdoings?

2. Is it possible for such organizations to prosper in the medium to long term?
3. Where leaders deliberately mislead staff and members of the public, what suitable action should be taken against such leaders?

III

The Rationale of Servant-Leadership

Preamble

The following discussion of servant-leadership is based on a speech I delivered at the Greenleaf Servant-Leadership UK Conference in 2002 entitled *I Remain, Sir, Your Obedient Servant,* a section from my inaugural professorial lecture *If at First You Don't Succeed...,* a public lecture I delivered at the University of Oxford, *Vocation in Business and Industry* and an extract from a book of mine, *Effective People.*[1]

The four different sources, and possibly three different styles, have been brought together into one coherent account of why I find servant-leadership a most intriguing topic. I believe this blend of materials will challenge the inquiring reader and provide further insight into both the principles and application of servant-leadership. Much of what follows is based on the spoken word and therefore will involve a different style from what has gone before.

Introduction

Most of the great religions of the world reserve a special place in their heart for the convert, especially those converts who have come to faith somewhat late in life. The convert's stumbling discovery of the truth is celebrated and encouraged. Obvious gaps in knowledge—and sometimes these gaps amount to alarming chasms—are glossed over with benign and understanding smiles; their very words, their testimony, are an encouragement to those who have practiced and studied the faith for decades if not generations.

I do not want to suggest that servant-leadership is a religion, to be compared with Christianity, Judaism, Islam or some other faith, although I will imply later that there is an inspirational, even spiritual dimension to the writings and work on servant-leadership. Neither will I claim that you come to a belief in servant-leadership through faith, but I do believe that the metaphor of a convert is an apt description of the journey I have been on for the best part of thirty years.

Whenever I speak at a conference, the use of this convert metaphor invokes certain sympathy in my audience. It also allows me to look to those experienced "in the faith" and encourage them to celebrate even my stumbling discoveries and be encouraged that someone such as I, a fairly hard-nosed former executive, has discovered the truth of servant-leadership...at last.

It is important for me to say something briefly about my career to date and to explain the comment "someone such as I." At present I am professor of leadership and organization development within a university business school, and prior to that I was the founding chief executive of the National Health Service Staff College Wales, an organization committed to helping people from all parts of the service and all professions to learn, develop, and lead. I have also been director of manpower services for NHS Wales, an organization with more than seventy thousand staff, and in my manufacturing days I was an industrial relations manager in heavy industry and became a program director at the industry's national training and development college. From my early experiences as a manager I was totally committed to the notion (and continue to be) that organizations need to be run efficiently and effectively.

The job titles I held are of little importance. What is far more important is that, in each and every job I did, I was committed to the way in which the people of the organization were developed. One boss even called me a zealot. In some jobs it was easier to demonstrate that fact and in others, especially those concerned with the hurly-burly of industrial relations in the late 1970s, it was much harder, if not impossible.

Throughout my working life, as a part of my commitment to people and their development, I have made sure that my reading and academic studies have supported my belief in the development of people. So you can imagine the joy I felt when I came across the writings of Robert Greenleaf, Larry Spears, and many others on servant-leadership. What surprised me most of all is that their books hadn't landed on my desk much earlier. After reading them I felt a little like M. Jourdain, one of Molière's characters, who in a discussion with a professor of philosophy made a great discovery and exclaimed, "Good heavens! For more than forty years I have been speaking prose without knowing it."

The Persuasive Case for Servant Leadership

As one reads through the servant-leadership literature, the inexpert reader is extremely grateful to discover the way in which Larry Spears, the chief executive of the Greenleaf Center in the United States and the headquarters for the worldwide network of Greenleaf centers, has taken the ideas central to servant-leadership and codified the key principles into ten characteristics.[2] What follows is an abridged version of Larry Spears's perceptive insight:

1. *Listening*: "...a deep commitment to listening intently to others....They seek to listen receptively to what is being said (and not being said!). Listening also involves getting in touch with one's own inner voice...listening, coupled with regular periods of reflection, are essential to the growth of the servant-leader."
2. *Empathy:* "...striving to understand and empathize with others. People need to be accepted and recognized for their special and unique spirits. One must assume the good intentions of co-workers and not reject them as people, even when forced to reject their behavior or performance."
3. *Healing:* "Learning to heal is a powerful force for transformation and integration. One of the great strengths of

servant-leadership is the potential for healing one's self and others...."

4. *Awareness:* "General awareness, and especially self-awareness, strengthens the servant-leader....Awareness...aids in understanding issues involving ethics and values."

5. *Persuasion:* "...a reliance upon persuasion, rather than positional authority, in making decisions within an organization...the servant-leader is effective at building consensus within groups."

6. *Conceptualization:* "Servant-leaders seek to nurture their abilities to 'dream great dreams.' The ability to look at a problem...from a conceptualizing perspective means that one must think beyond day-to-day realities...a manager who wishes to be a servant-leader must stretch his or her thinking to encompass broader-based conceptual thinking."

7. *Foresight:* "The ability to foresee the likely outcome of a situation is hard to define, but easy to identify....Foresight is a characteristic that enables servant-leaders to understand the lessons from the past, the realities of the present, and the likely consequence of a decision for the future. It is deeply rooted within the intuitive mind."

8. *Stewardship:* "...[means] 'holding something in trust for another.' Robert Greenleaf's view of all institutions was one in which CEOs, staffs, directors, and trustees all played significant roles in holding their institutions in trust for the greater good of society."

9. *Commitment to the growth of people:* "...people have an intrinsic value beyond their tangible contributions as workers. As such, servant-leaders are deeply committed to the personal, professional, and spiritual growth of each and every individual within the institution."

10. *Building community:* "...servant-leaders seek to identify a means for building community among those who work within a given institution."

As I read the various servant-leadership books and reflected on their messages, four main reasons emerged that convinced me of the merits of servant-leadership. I want to look briefly at each of these four reasons and encourage you to continue your reflection in this most important of areas.

The first reason I shall call the inspirational evidence.

If you are a bibliophile like me, you cannot go many weeks without buying a book. My study shelves are straining under the weight of just the leadership, learning, and development books I have bought (and read) in the past few years. Some of the books are acknowledged classics in the field, others are little gems that one day will achieve classic status, and some, I have to confess, are unlikely to be opened ever again. In the categories of classics and gems are authors such as Peter Senge, Warren Bennis, Rosabeth Moss Kanter, and many others. As I read their books I noticed that time and again I would come across phrases such as these:

> For many years I have told people that although there are a lot of books on leadership, there is only one that serious students have to read—*Servant Leadership* by Robert K. Greenleaf...few [other books] penetrate to deeper insights into the nature of real leadership.... [Greenleaf] says that the first and most important choice a leader makes is the choice to serve, without which one's capacity to lead is profoundly limited. That choice is not an action in the normal sense—it's not something you do, but an expression of your being. —Peter Senge[3]
>
> I am a fan of Robert Greenleaf and think that servant leadership is the foundation for effective leadership.... —Ken Blanchard[4]
>
> ...servant leadership is the enabling art to accomplishing any worthy objective. —Stephen Covey[5]
>
> This is a wonderful book [referring to *Leadership Is an Art* by Max DePree]...it says more about leadership... than many of the much longer books that have been published on the subject. —Peter Drucker[6]

I could quote many other examples, but I hope these few quotations will illustrate my first reason. The writings of Robert Greenleaf and the concept of servant-leadership have impressed and had a profound effect on many of those people who now, in this generation, are seen as leading authorities in their field. I found the writings to be inspirational; I had to find out more.

My second reason is the business case.

There is always a danger in highlighting a glowing example of a certain principle or approach. Peters and Waterman discovered that after they launched their seminal work *In Search of Excellence*.[7] No sooner had they extolled the virtues of particular companies than some of those very companies went into decline, terminal decline in certain instances, not that that had anything to do with Peters and Waterman of course. However, the principles they discovered have stood the test of time and are now an accepted part of management practice.

In an even more profound way, the same is true with servant-leadership. I know little about U.S. companies such as TDIndustries, Southwest Airlines, Synovus Financial Corporation, Herman Miller Inc., and the other oft-quoted examples of servant-leadership in action, but you would have to possess the head-in-the-sand qualities of an ostrich to ignore the evidence from these organizations. It is surely far more than a coincidence that these companies often score well in the Fortune lists of "best companies to work for": In a sense, their employees provide proof for the business case, alongside the business and financial performance evidence. To pay no attention to the fast-growing various pieces of evidence seems to me to commit the folly of our forebears who ignored the total quality revolution occurring in the Far East until it was almost too late.

Then there is the growing, but infant, evidence from UK-based companies. In a recent book, Judith Leary-Joyce,[8] a fellow member of the Greenleaf Centre for Servant-Leadership UK, shows that servant-leadership is alive and kicking in the UK. Her research was conducted among companies scoring highly in the "Sunday Times 100 Best Companies to Work For" poll. Leary-Joyce asked various companies, "What do great leaders do, and how does servant-leadership meet a healthy bottom-line?" and discovered a significant number of those companies—companies such as Honda, Asda, Flight Centre, Hiscocks and Corgi—practicing some form of servant-leadership, even if in many instances they did so without making much of a song and dance about it. They often avoided any jargon surrounding the concept, but clearly many of their management practices were directly influenced, even governed, by the principles of servant-leadership.

I confess to being intrigued by many new "-isms" in the world of business, its people, and their development, but no one can argue that the concept of servant-leadership is some new idea, or passing fad. It is something that has stood the test of time. Neither can it be said that servant-leadership does not make good business sense: Greenleaf and others recognized that in all organizations hard decisions have to be taken and employees have to understand what they are expected to deliver. Servant-leadership does not contradict the basic rigors of business life but it does fundamentally influence the way in which business practice is conducted.

The moral case is my third reason.

Throughout my working life I have been appalled, and I use the word advisedly, by the manner in which some managers have treated their employees. It seems that Henry Ford's alleged maxim, "Why is it that whenever I ask for a pair of hands, a brain comes attached?" is alive and well in far too many companies. I well remember my first experience of this: When I started work in the manufacturing sector I met a man I had known all my life and whom I shall call David Jackson. He worked, I learned to my dismay, as a sweeper: He spent all day brushing up the mess left by other workers. Yet this man was a respected pillar of his community, someone to whom people looked up, someone who could be relied on for his wisdom and judgment, and someone who exercised valuable leadership within his church.

Max DePree memorably addresses this very principle in *Leadership Is an Art*[9] by quoting the poet Thomas Gray to lament the fact that "talent may go unnoticed and unused" and that:

Full many a gem of purest ray serene,
The dark unfathomed caves of ocean bear:
Full many a flower is born to blush unseen,
And waste its sweetness on the desert air.

I know that servant-leadership is not a philanthropic movement established to liberate all and sundry from every menial task, but the reason David Jackson's qualities were not used by that company was due to senior management's belief that manual grades had little, if anything, to offer the organization. This is such a waste of human talent. I believe we have a moral duty to treat people with respect, to make use of the potential within them, to develop their contribution, to see them as partners within the organization (I use the word *partners* in the stakeholder sense of the word), and to realize that serving their interests is consistent with serving the needs of the organization.

I cannot emphasize this moral point too much. Recently, I read the autobiography of Jack Welch,[10] the former CEO of General Electric, whom *Fortune* called the greatest manager of the twentieth century. The book is an exciting tale of how he transformed the performance of the company, a highly commendable act, and it stands as a textbook to be read by anyone interested in the role of management. However, it is also clear why he inherited the sobriquet Neutron Jack as he purged the organization of layer after layer of management. He would seize any concept to improve the bottom-line performance of the company (and many were commendable actions in my view), and, no doubt, he would have taken hold of the concept of servant-leadership if someone had shown him that it would improve profitability. But that misses the point as far as I am concerned: While there is a business case reason for servant-leadership, to apply the concept without any recognition of the moral imperative (if that is indeed what Welch would have done) shows little understanding of its key principles.

My fourth and final reason is the evidence from human nature.

I can sum up this point in three words by saying, "Because people respond!" People are amazing, and they constantly surprise you, and themselves, by what they are able to achieve if you allow them to operate under appropriate conditions. I could tell you story after story of people who appear to "grow" before your very eyes when placed in the right environment. What is true for individuals is also true for groups of people and is also true for organizations as a whole. But with organizations it is much harder. It seems that senior people find it hard to believe that what they know to be true for individuals, and have seen happening for groups, can also be used to transform their organization.

One of my favorite quotes comes from *A Return to Love* by Marianne Williamson—a quote, incidentally, that is often erroneously attributed to Nelson Mandela's inaugural speech—and the words seem so appropriate to illustrate this final reason.

Our deepest fear is not that we are inadequate.

Our deepest fear is that we are powerful beyond measure.

It is our light not our darkness, that most frightens us.

We ask ourselves, who am I to be brilliant, gorgeous, talented and famous?

Actually, who are you not to be?

You are a child of God. Your playing small doesn't serve the world. There is nothing enlightened about shrinking so that other people won't feel insecure around you.

We were born to magnify the glory of God that is within us.

It's not just in some of us; it's in everyone.

And as we let our own light shine, we unconsciously give other people permission to do the same.

As we are liberated from our own fear, our presence automatically liberates others.

I can think of no better way to encourage people to show others the amazing talents that they possess.

As I work with people across this country, I often see a self-imposed reticence, a reluctance and hesitancy to realize and capitalize upon the amazing talents that lie within them. What we need are leaders who are willing to stand up and become servants—servant-leaders. And we need people who are prepared to accept the leadership that is being offered to them.

So there you have it, the four main reasons why I am pleased to associate myself with servant-leadership: the inspirational evidence, the business case, the moral case, and the evidence from human nature.

Some Misunderstandings Along the Way

Taking the concept of servant-leadership on board and making it the philosophy by which I tried to lead an organization was not easy sailing. There were misunderstandings, obstacles, and people's objections to overcome along the way.

The first misunderstanding was all my own work! I have to confess that the first time I read Robert Greenleaf's book I thought it to be a rather sentimental work. Although I warmed to his affirmation that "I am in the business of growing people—people who are stronger, healthier, more autonomous, more self-reliant, more competent," I was puzzled by the almost offhand way in which he added, "Incidentally, we also make and sell at a profit things that people want to buy so we can pay for all of this."

It appealed to the near-cavalier spirit within me but I found little in it to fit in with the "real world," and it would have been impossible to convince my business-driven colleagues to try to apply such principles. However, the notions contained in his words, "one way that some people serve is to lead," and his belief of a society where "the more able serve the less able" were tantalizingly attractive propositions.

The reason for my misunderstanding is that I failed to understand that servant-leadership is not an alternative, quasi–New Age, system where the needs of people are paramount and bottom-line performance of the business is of little relevance, or a coincidental outcome of treating staff decently and with dignity. As I read other writers it dawned on me that servant-leadership, business efficiency, and sound management practice were not mutually exclusive concepts.

For this insight I am grateful to people such as Max DePree,[11] who wrote, "...liberating people to do what is required of them in the most effective and humane way possible"; to Ken Blanchard,[12] who, in correcting someone's misunderstanding of servant-leadership, wrote, "...their assumption when they heard the term was that managers should be working for their people, who would be deciding what to do, when to do it, and how to do it. If that was what servant leadership was all about, it didn't sound to them like leadership at all. It sounded more like the inmates were running the prison. I think it's important for us to correct this misconception. Leadership has two aspects—a visionary part and an implementation part"; and to Larry Spears[13] for showing that "...servant-leadership emphasizes increased service to others, a holistic approach to work, building a sense of community, and the sharing of power in decision making."

These writers recognized that there are times in all organizations when hard decisions have to be taken and employees need to be shown clearly what they are expected to deliver. I realized that servant-leadership does not contradict the basic rigors of business but influences the way in which business is conducted.

Other misunderstandings were chiefly the work of my colleagues. One colleague, a chief executive of a government-funded agency, declared that as he was both a public servant and a leader then obviously he was a servant-leader. Not only did he misunderstand the ethos of servant-leadership but his leadership practice in that organization was the very antithesis of the principles espoused by Greenleaf and others. In terms of the traditional boss as opposed to the servant as leader, set out helpfully in McGee-Cooper and Looper's volume,[14] he operated in a highly competitive manner, used fear and intimidation to get what he wanted, controlled information in order to maintain power, used internal politics for personal gain, and viewed accountability as a means to assign blame. Some servant-leader!

Yet, this presents something of a dilemma. On the one hand, if you are attempting to develop the concept of servant-leadership in your organization, should you be grateful to anyone who appears to be lending support to your ideas? On the other hand, it is perfectly understandable to be alarmed that the unattractive style of management, and a style counter to the principles of servant-leadership, will actually alienate the very people you are trying to influence. A thorny problem, so what do you do? Tackle the problem head-on and potentially create a hostile environment or ignore the issue in the hope that the boorish individual will disappear into the undergrowth?

Another manager, who heard me speaking about servant-leadership at a conference, saw an opportunity to gain access to what she erroneously believed to be the corridors of power. She wanted to develop her career and was continually on the lookout for the latest thinking, any new ideas being discussed by senior management, so that she could use them as a shibboleth in her quest for career development. With this sort of person any newly heard approach would do as long as it served her short and medium term career aspirations. I do not wish to appear harsh in my description of her; in many ways I admired her determination and motivation. But it does raise a further dilemma: There is an understandable temptation to see the concept of servant-leadership as something so important that one has to do all one can to retain the purity of the message (again, I am trespassing into the territory of religious belief). At the same time, if one engages in proselytizing, spreading the message, then, inevitably, new adherents may use areas of servant-leadership for their own ends. It's a matter of purity versus popularity at the end of the day, I guess.

My final example of misunderstanding is taken from the world of academia. One of my university colleagues appeared to think I had taken leave of my senses and very *helpfully* e-mailed me a copy of an article written by Russell and Stone, two U.S. academics.[15] In their article they used a forensic and somewhat mechanical approach to question the very foundations of servant-leadership. The article was entertaining, well researched, and an important contribution to the debate, although the two writers appeared not to have got to the very heart of the servant-leadership message. However, what it does show is the importance of stimulating the debate on servant-leadership, of producing further examples of its success, of stimulating research, and of encouraging the emergence of even more apologists for the concept.

Toward a Conclusion

For me, all four reasons for my belief in servant-leadership are fundamentally important and, again for me, I cannot see how the concept can exist and be relevant without all four of them being present.

First, there is a need to appreciate how servant-leadership has inspired other people, especially those who have had such a profound impact on the development of others. Also, it is essential to allow its inspirational qualities to influence the way in which each one of us practices our leadership roles.

Second, there is a need to recognize that profitable companies are the bedrock upon which much of the remainder of society is founded. Without their contribution, education, health, the arts, and much else would be in a parlous state. So servant-leadership is, and should be, inextricably connected to the performance of the company.

Third, there is a need to treat people with dignity and respect. Hanging on my office wall is a copy of the International Charter for Human Rights, a powerful reminder of these principles and something inherently a part of servant-leadership.

Fourth, there is a need to share experiences of how people respond positively to its practice in order to demonstrate that servant-leadership can be applied successfully.

IV
Conclusion

You know, as well as I do, that leading a group of people or an organization is a tough job with many highs and lows and a seemingly constant stream of challenges. We also know that when a writer attempts to boil leadership down into three or four easy steps those writers demonstrate their inexperience, if not their naïveté.

The last thing anyone can say about this book is that it attempts to make leadership sound simple and straightforward. It treats leadership as a complex, even though rewarding, activity and offers thoughts, suggestions, and principles to help the leader reflect on their servant-leadership role and, hopefully, improve the way it is practiced. In so doing, readers will find greater reward for themselves and the people they lead.

It is for this reason that the concluding chapter of the book is short. Enough has been said: The book is there to make you think, to stimulate discussion, to encourage and perhaps even infuriate, but, above all, the book is there to champion the cause of servant-leadership and to shed light on that concept from the abundance of stories and teaching in the Bible.

I wish you well in your journey. May your servant-leadership become a source of joy for you in your work and personal life.

Appendix
Biblical References and Synopsis of Material

The Nature and Qualities of Servant-Leadership

REFERENCE 1: 1 PETER 5:1–11

The apostle Peter sets out the qualities and role of elders and young men in the young church and, by implication, throughout the centuries since.

REFERENCE 2: EXODUS 34:29–32

Moses descends from Mount Sinai with new tablets of stone and his face is shining. Moses calls Aaron and the leaders and speaks to them; then he calls all of the people and gives them commandments from God.

REFERENCE 3: MATTHEW 15:8–14

Jesus points out to the Pharisees their hypocrisy ("honors me with their lips") and condemns them for being the "blind guides of the blind."

REFERENCE 4: PHILIPPIANS 1:9–11

The apostle Paul sets out for the young church at Philippi some qualities appropriate for leadership, for example, love, knowledge, insight, purity, blamelessness.

Reference 5: 1 Timothy 3:1–13

The apostle Paul instructs the young leader Timothy on the qualities needed to become an overseer or deacon.

Reference 6: 1 Timothy 5—6

Paul gives a more detailed charge to Timothy, parts of which have a resonance with leadership.

Reference 7: Titus 1:6–16

The apostle Paul sets out a list of attributes for elders, the leaders in the church.

Reference 8: Exodus 18:15–26

Moses is swamped by his workload as the people he is leading are coming to him for every decision. His father-in-law tells him that this pressure cannot continue, as he will wear himself out. He advises Moses to deal only with the major issues. He should teach the people the laws, how to live, and the duties they should undertake. He should select capable men from among the people and appoint them to oversee the work of thousands, hundreds, fifties, and tens.

Reference 9: Numbers 36

Moses set out rules for the disposal of land, but the representatives of Zelophehad's daughters ask him to change the rules to meet their circumstances—new circumstances that hadn't been envisaged. Moses listens and issues revised instructions.

Reference 10: Deuteronomy 1:9–18

In an account similar to Exodus 18 above, Moses tells the people that they are too heavy a burden for him to carry alone, as their numbers have increased greatly. He asks them to choose "individuals who are wise, discerning, and reputable to be your leaders." He appoints them over thousands, hundreds, fifties, and tens. The leaders should act fairly, without partiality, treat everyone the same, and pass on to Moses the "too hard" cases.

REFERENCE 11: NUMBERS 11:16–18

The Lord says to Moses to bring seventy elders/leaders to the tent of meeting so that they can stand with him. The Lord says he will come and speak and "take some of the spirit that is on you and put it on them." The result is that they will help Moses carry the burden. The Lord challenges the people about their attitude and their view that they had been better off in Egypt.

REFERENCE 12: NUMBERS 34:18–28

God tells Moses to appoint men to assign the land for him. It appears that there are two special deputies: Eleazar the priest and Joshua. Also, there is one man from each of the tribes.

REFERENCE 13: DEUTERONOMY 33:21

Moses is discussing his various leaders and praises Gad (this is not a typo: I do mean Gad!) who "chose the best for himself" and acknowledges that it was the leader's portion. He also compliments Gad for carrying out the right actions.

REFERENCE 14: EZEKIEL 17:12–14

The king of Babylon goes to Jerusalem and captures the king and his nobles and also takes away the leading men. The result is that "the kingdom might be humble and not lift itself up, and that by keeping his covenant it might stand."

REFERENCE 15: ROMANS 12:3–8

This is one of three passages that set out the gifts given to the church by God.

The Work of a Servant-Leader

REFERENCE 16: NUMBERS 7:2–3, 10–11

The leaders bring offerings to present at the tabernacle before its dedication. This was a daily event involving one leader.

REFERENCE 17: 2 SAMUEL 12:15–17

The child of Uriah's wife and David is very ill and eventually dies. David is distraught, prays for the child, and fasts; the elders stand by and support him.

REFERENCE 18: 1 TIMOTHY 4:14–15

The apostle Paul writes to Timothy, a young man, and encourages him not to neglect his gift (which includes leadership) and to be diligent.

REFERENCE 19: NUMBERS 13:2—14:38

Moses sends one leader from each tribe to explore Canaan. Moses gives instructions about how to get to Canaan. The spies are to report on the land and people, the towns and defenses, and the fertility of the land. They come back and report that the land is fruitful but the people are powerful. Caleb silences the others and argues that they should take the land, but the others contend that they cannot attack, as the others are far stronger. Those opposed to Caleb's view start spreading rumors.

REFERENCE 20: JOSHUA 7:1—8:29

Achan steals possessions that should have been given to God. Achan is then involved in planning the battle strategy to win Ai. Things go horribly wrong: They lose the battle and many comrades are killed. Joshua is devastated, since he had expected to win Ai easily, as his strategists had told him. Joshua eventually realizes that the issue will only be resolved by finding the culprit (Achan) and dealing with him. Devising new strategies and tactics, Joshua leads the attack, taking with him the whole army and the best leaders, and they win a famous victory in Ai.

REFERENCE 21: ECCLESIASTES 1:1, 12:8

The Teacher realizes and exclaims that everything is meaningless: "Vanity of vanities...all is vanity."

REFERENCE 22: JOEL 1:2–12

Joel tells the people to wake up and realize that a swarm of locusts has stripped them bare and caused ruin. There seems to be lethargy; they need to wake up, take action, and not just mourn for their loss.

REFERENCE 23: JOSHUA 9

When the Gibeonites hear about Joshua's victories, they want to form an alliance with him. They pretend to be from a distant country and to be in need of his protection because of their adversities. They say they will be his servants. Joshua enters into a peace treaty with them and then finds out that he has been deceived—they were neighbors and not from a far land. The assembly grumbles against their leaders, but Joshua keeps his treaty, although he makes the Gibeonites work as woodcutters and water carriers.

REFERENCE 24: ACTS 15:1-21

Some teachers say that Gentile Christians need to be circumcised. Paul and Barnabas disagree with them. To resolve the issue, they bring it before the apostles and elders in Jerusalem. The council considers the points made and James issues a clear policy: There is no need for them to be circumcised, but they should obey certain laws concerning idols, food, and sex. James says he will write to them.

REFERENCE 25: NUMBERS 16

Korah and others decide to challenge the leadership of Moses and Aaron. The group of challengers includes 250 well-known community leaders who claim that Moses has "gone too far" and that, unnecessarily, he sets himself apart from the other leaders. Moses summons two men who complain about the desert conditions and accuse Moses of exalting himself "above the assembly of the Lord." Moses sets up a challenge, in which God shows clearly that Moses is his man. Despite this clear demonstration there still remained "mumblers" and "groaners."

REFERENCE 26: JEREMIAH 19:1–13

The Lord says to buy a clay jar and to go out and warn the people that, since they have departed from his ways, they can expect a disaster. The jar is smashed as a warning to them that a similar fate awaits them and their environment.

REFERENCE 27: NUMBERS 25:1–4

In this dramatic passage, the men become sexually immoral, sacrifice to idols, and worship Baal. God is angry and tells Moses to take the leaders and kill them.

REFERENCE 28: NUMBERS 31:13–20

Moses is angry that his orders have not been carried out fully. He issues new orders and gets the men to purify themselves and their weapons.

REFERENCE 29: DEUTERONOMY 27:15–26

A series of curses reminds those in positions of authority of their responsibilities.

REFERENCE 30: DEUTERONOMY 29:9-12

God renews the covenant with his people and tells them to follow the terms carefully so that they may prosper.

REFERENCE 31: ACTS 20:17–21

The apostle Paul calls together the Ephesian elders, justifies his past actions, and tells them of his future plans. He shows that everything has been done to fulfill the task given to him.

REFERENCE 32: 1 KINGS 12:1–19

The people ask Rehoboam, the successor of his father Solomon as king of Israel, for a lighter burden. He consults the elders, rejects their advice, and then consults his young friends. He follows their advice to make the burden harder. Rehoboam eventually experiences serious problems, and the united kingdom of David and Solomon is divided into two kingdoms.

REFERENCE 33: 1 CHRONICLES 12:23–37

This is the story of the men from the tribes coming to support David in his battle against Saul. The men are listed by tribe and number and some of their attributes are given.

REFERENCE 34: PSALMS 119:99–100

The psalmist claims to have "more understanding than all my teachers" and to "understand more than the aged."

REFERENCE 35: ISAIAH 40:11

This passage describes the leader as a shepherd with special responsibility to take care of lambs and gently lead those who have young.

REFERENCE 36: JOHN 10:1–5

The sheep know the voice of the shepherd and follow him.

REFERENCE 37: ACTS 20:28–31

Paul tells the elders of the church to keep watch and to be aware that "wolves will come in" and from within the church there will be people who will try to distort the truth. Be on your guard. Paul spent three years warning them.

Reference 38: Deuteronomy 27:1–3

Moses tells the people that when they enter the promised land they must keep all of the commands and write all the words of the law on large stones coated with plaster. They must adhere to them.

Reference 39: 1 Kings 21:5–16

In this story of Naboth's vineyard, Jezebel acts on Ahab's behalf, has Naboth killed (on the basis of trumped-up evidence), and gets the vineyards for Ahab.

Reference 40: Ezra 5

When Haggai and his associates start to rebuild the Temple, they are challenged over the source of their authority to do this. The officials send a letter to King Darius informing him of Haggai's work and asking whether he approves. King Darius gives his approval.

Reference 41: Matthew 21:23

The priests challenge Jesus over the authority he has to undertake his ministry.

Reference 42: 1 Samuel 4

The Philistines capture the ark and the Israelites try to learn lessons from their defeat.

Reference 43: 2 Chronicles 28:12–15

Some leaders in Ephraim confront those arriving from war and say, "You shall not bring the captives in here," as it would add to their guilt before God.

Reference 44: Ezra 8:15–17

Ezra brings together a number of leaders as well as Joiarab and Elnathan "who were wise."

REFERENCE 45: 1 CHRONICLES 29:6–9

David begins the process of handing over the throne to Solomon. The leaders are supportive of David, but chiefly this account concerns the leaders giving willingly and generously to the cost of building the Temple.

REFERENCE 46: NEHEMIAH 12:24

The leaders of the Levites have associates who stand opposite them to give them praise and thanksgiving.

REFERENCE 47: ACTS 15:22–35 AND 16:4

The Council at Jerusalem sends representatives with Paul and Barnabas to tell the Gentile Christians the good news about their decision concerning religious practice. They communicate the news, and Paul and Barnabas remain there teaching and preaching. The decision is then communicated far and wide in the other towns.

The Appointment of Servant-Leaders and the Question of Succession

REFERENCE 48: NUMBERS 17:1–11

To show that Aaron is indeed a leader like his brother Moses, each of the leaders of the tribes has to leave his staff in the tent of meeting; the staff that sprouts would identify the true leader. Aaron's staff not only sprouted but also "put forth buds, produced blossoms, and bore ripe almonds."

REFERENCE 49: DEUTERONOMY 31:26–29

Moses calls the Levites who carried the ark and tells them that he knows how rebellious they have been and that he knows that when he (Moses) is gone they will "surely act corruptly, turning aside from the way that I have commanded you," and disaster will fall on them.

REFERENCE 50: JOSHUA 23:1–16 AND 24:1–27

Joshua is old and tells the elders and leaders, "I am about to go the way of all the earth." He reminds them that it is the Lord who has won the battles for them and reminds them to follow his ways. In a long speech, setting out their history and experiences, he challenges them: "choose this day whom you will serve."

REFERENCE 51: JUDGES 11:5–11

Jephthah is ostracized by his family and people because he is the product of his father's liaison with a prostitute. But Israel is being attacked by the Ammonites and they need Jephthah to lead them. He is wary of their approach but agrees to lead them after certain assurances are given.

REFERENCE 52: 1 SAMUEL 9:16—13:2, 14

The people want a king instead of the present system where God rules via the word of the prophets. Saul is anointed in preparation to becoming king, and when he is introduced to the people there is a sense of "there is no one like him among all the people." Saul starts to terrorize the people; he's then made king and, over time, things start to go wrong. Samuel rebukes Saul, and there is the emergence of David: "the LORD has sought out a man after his own heart." Fortunately, the people realize they have made a mistake with Saul. Things are put right and David is anointed king.

REFERENCE 53: 1 CHRONICLES 22:5–19 AND 28:4–21

Both stories concern David handing over the work of building the Temple to his son Solomon, of David reflecting on the lessons he has learned, advising Solomon on how he should behave, and telling the people to give Solomon every support.

REFERENCE 54: NEHEMIAH 9:17

This is an account of how Israel's forebears became arrogant, appointed the wrong leader(s), and as a result of their decision returned "to their slavery."

Servant-Leadership and Management

REFERENCE 55: NUMBERS 2, 33:1, 1 CHRONICLES 27:4, AND 2 CHRONICLES 26:12

These are four similar readings that deal with the organizational arrangement of men into divisions and the equipping of them for battle.

REFERENCE 56: NUMBERS 3:21–35

This is another list setting out various roles for people to undertake.

REFERENCE 57: 1 CHRONICLES 23:2

This is yet another section that sets out various roles and responsibilities.

REFERENCE 58: LUKE 12:42–48

This is the parable of the faithful and wise manager (servant).

REFERENCE 59: LUKE 16:1-13.

This is the parable of the unjust steward.

Servant-Leadership and Followers

REFERENCE 60: 1 SAMUEL 22:2

David escapes to the cave at Adullam and there he ends up leading "everyone who was in distress, and everyone who was in debt, and everyone who was discontented." There were about four hundred of them.

REFERENCE 61: 1 SAMUEL 30:1–24

David's camp at Ziklag has been overrun and his wives carried off. The men are angry with David and talk of stoning him. David gains strength from the Lord. They find out where their enemies are, and all of David's men, except two hundred who were too tired, give chase. They beat their enemies and plunder their riches. When it comes to sharing out the bounty, David insists that all, including those two hundred tired men who stayed behind to protect the camp, should have equal shares.

REFERENCE 62: JUDGES 2:8–19

While Joshua was alive the people served the Lord, but after his death "another generation grew up after them, who did not know the LORD or the work that he had done for Israel." They court disaster, and when God raises up judges they won't listen to them. They "abandoned the LORD."

REFERENCE 63: JUDGES 9:1–6

Abimelech is appointed the leader and then hires followers (lieutenants) who are "worthless and reckless fellows." He and they cause mayhem among the nations.

REFERENCE 64: 1 KINGS 16:21–22

The followers of Omri were stronger than those of his challengers, "and Omri became king."

REFERENCE 65: 1 CHRONICLES 12:18–22

Amasai and his men align themselves with David, who uses them as his raiding party. Many other groups defect to David and David ends up with a "great army."

REFERENCE 66: LUKE 22:47–49

This recounts Judas's kiss of betrayal.

REFERENCE 67: ACTS 9:20–30

The apostle Paul escapes from his enemies at Damascus in a basket through an opening in the wall.

REFERENCE 68: HEBREWS 13:17

The author declares it is the duty of followers to "obey your leaders and submit to them."

REFERENCE 69: HEBREWS 13:7

The author says leaders need to set an example, and he admonishes followers, "Remember your leaders...consider the outcome of their way of life."

When Leadership Goes Wrong

REFERENCE 70: LEVITICUS 4:22–24

This passage covers the unintentional sins of a leader and a system of sacrifice by which the priest makes atonement for the sins.

REFERENCE 71: 2 CHRONICLES 36:11–14

This is the account of Zedekiah, a bad king, and the poor influence he had upon the other people.

REFERENCE 72: EZRA 9

The leaders come to Ezra and tell him that the people have acted detestably by marrying their neighbors. What is worse is that it was the leaders who led them into these practices. Ezra offers a prayer of confession, they clear out all of the bad practices, and everyone is summoned to Jerusalem (and they will be punished if they are not there in three days) to hear the "riot act" being read.

REFERENCE 73: NEHEMIAH 9:32–38

The people have become slaves because their leaders did not follow the commands of God. The people are suffering because of the neglect of their leaders.

REFERENCE 74: ISAIAH 3:14–15

The Lord enters into judgment against the elders and the leaders because of what they have done.

REFERENCE 75: JEREMIAH 5

This is a prophecy based on the notion, "if you can find one person who acts justly." There is widespread corruption and even the leaders have sold out.

REFERENCE 76: EZEKIEL 11:1–12

Ezekiel prophesies against wicked leaders and tells them of the doom to come.

REFERENCE 77: MICAH 3

Micah rebukes evil leaders and prophets and tells them they will be punished.

REFERENCE 78: ACTS 3:17–19

Brothers who acted in ignorance are given the opportunity to repent and to experience "times of refreshing."

REFERENCE 79: ACTS 13:50

The leading men are stirred up to oppose Paul and Barnabas and to expel them from their region.

Notes

Chapter 1

1. Robert K. Greenleaf, "Lessons on Power," in *On Becoming a Servant Leader: The Private Writings of Robert K. Greenleaf,* ed. Don M. Frick and Larry C. Spears (San Francisco: Jossey-Bass, 1996), 155.

2. Robert K. Greenleaf, *Servant Leadership: A Journey into the Nature of Legitimate Power and Greatness* (New York/Mahwah, NJ: Paulist Press, 1997).

3. Robert K. Greenleaf, *The Servant Leader Within,* ed. Hamilton Beazley, Julie Beggs, and Larry C. Spears (New York/Mahwah, NJ: Paulist Press, 2003), 248.

4. Anne T. Fraker and Larry C. Spears, *Seeker and Servant: Reflections in Religious Leadership* (San Francisco: Jossey-Bass, 1996).

5. Robert K. Greenleaf, "The Practice of Openness," in *On Becoming a Servant Leader: The Private Writings of Robert K. Greenleaf,* ed. Don M. Frick and Larry C. Spears (San Francisco: Jossey-Bass, 1996), chapter 6.

6. Robert K. Greenleaf, "Entheos and Growth," in *On Becoming a Servant Leader: The Private Writings of Robert K. Greenleaf,* ed. Don M. Frick and Larry C. Spears (San Francisco: Jossey-Bass, 1996), chapter 8.

7. Robert K. Greenleaf, "Coercion, Manipulation, and Persuasion," in *On Becoming a Servant Leader: The Private Writings of Robert K. Greenleaf,* ed. Don M. Frick and Larry C. Spears (San Francisco: Jossey-Bass, 1996), 127.

8. Robert K. Greenleaf, "The Servant as Leader," in Robert K. Greenleaf, *The Servant Leader Within,* ed. Hamilton Beazley,

Julie Beggs, and Larry C. Spears (New York/Mahwah, NJ: Paulist Press, 2003).

9. Ken Blanchard, "The Heart of Servant-Leadership," in *Focus on Leadership*, ed. Larry C. Spears and Michele Lawrence (New York: John Wiley and Sons, 2002), foreword.

10. Ken Blanchard, "Servant-Leadership Revisited," in *Insights on Leadership*, ed. Larry C. Spears (New York: John Wiley and Sons, 1998).

11. James A. Autry, *The Servant Leader* (Roseville, CA: Prima Publishing, 2001).

12. James A. Autry, *Love and Profit: The Art of Caring Leadership* (New York: Avon Books, 1991).

13. Bill Bottum with Dorothy Lenz, "Within Our Reach: Servant-Leadership for the Twenty-first Century," in *Insights on Leadership*, ed. Larry C. Spears (New York: John Wiley and Sons, 1998).

14. David L. Specht with Richard R. Broholm, "Toward a Theology of Institutions," in *Practicing Servant Leadership*, ed. Larry C. Spears and Michele Lawrence (San Francisco: Jossey-Bass, 2004).

15. Joseph D. DiStefano, "Tracing the Vision and Impact of Robert K. Greenleaf," in *Reflections on Leadership: How Robert K. Greenleaf's Theory of Servant-Leadership Influenced Today's Top Management Thinkers*, ed. Larry C. Spears (New York: John Wiley and Sons, 1995).

16. Carl Reiser, "Claiming Servant-Leadership as Your Heritage," in *Reflections on Leadership: How Robert K. Greenleaf's Theory of Servant-Leadership Influenced Today's Top Management Thinkers*, ed. Larry C. Spears (New York: John Wiley and Sons, 1995).

17. Ronald A. Heifetz, *Leadership Without Easy Answers* (Cambridge, MA: The Belknap Press of Harvard University Press, 1994).

18. Stephen W. Prosser conference lectures: *Vocation in Business and Industry*, University of Oxford, *If at First You Don't Succeed*, University of Glamorgan. Available from author.

19. Robert K. Greenleaf, *Servant Leadership: A Journey into the Nature of Legitimate Power and Greatness* (New York/Mahwah, NJ: Paulist Press, 1997).

Chapter 3

1. Stephen W. Prosser, *Effective People: Leadership and Organisation Development in Healthcare* (Oxford: Radcliffe Publishing, 2005).

2. Larry C. Spears, "Tracing the Past, Present, and Future of Servant-Leadership," in *Focus on Leadership*, ed. Larry C. Spears and Michele Lawrence (New York, John Wiley and Sons, 2002), introduction.

3. Peter Senge, "Introduction," in *Synchronicity—the Inner Path of Leadership*, by Joseph Jaworski (San Francisco: Berrett-Koehler Publishers, 1996).

4. Ken Blanchard, "Foreword," in *Focus on Leadership*, ed. Larry C. Spears and Michele Lawrence (New York: John Wiley and Sons, 2002).

5. Stephen R. Covey, "Servant-Leadership and Community Leadership in the Twenty-first Century," in *Focus on Leadership*, ed. Larry C. Spears and Michele Lawrence (New York: John Wiley and Sons, 2002).

6. Peter F. Drucker's testimonial for Max DePree, *Leadership Is an Art* (London: Dell Trade Paperback, 1990).

7. Thomas H. Peters and Robert H. Waterman, *In Search of Excellence* (New York: Harper and Row, 1986).

8. Judith Leary-Joyce, *Becoming an Employer of Choice* (London: Chartered Institute of Personnel and Development, 2004).

9. Max DePree, *Leadership Is an Art* (New York: Doubleday, 1989).

10. Jack Welch, with John A. Byrne, *Jack* (London: Headline Book Publishing, 2001).

11. Max DePree,. *Leadership Is an Art* (New York: Doubleday, 1989).

12. Ken Blanchard, "Foreword," in *Focus on Leadership*, ed. Larry C. Spears and Michele Lawrence (New York: John Wiley and Sons, 2002).

13. Larry Spears, "Introduction," in *Focus on Leadership*, ed. Larry C. Spears and Michele Lawrence (New York: John Wiley and Sons, 2002).

14. Ann McGee-Cooper and Gary Looper, *The Essentials of Servant-Leadership: Principles in Practice* (Waltham, MA: Pegasus Communications, Inc., 2001).

15. Robert F. Russell and A. Gregory Stone, "A Review of Servant Leadership Attributes: Developing a Practical Model," *Leadership and Organisation Development Journal*, March 23, 2002.